KNACK®
MAKE IT EASY

COACHING
YOUTH SOCCER

KNACK®

COACHING
YOUTH SOCCER

Step-by-Step Instruction on Strategy, Mechanic, Drills, and Winning

D.W. CRISFIELD

Photography by Beth Balbierz

KNACK®
MAKE IT EASY

Guilford, Connecticut
An imprint of The Globe Pequot Press

Copyright © 2009 by Morris Book Publishing, LLC

Editor-in-Chief: Maureen Graney
Editor: Katie Benoit
Cover Design: Paul Beatrice, Bret Kerr
Text Design: Paul Beatrice
Layout: Kevin Mak
Cover photos by Beth Balbierz
All interior photos by Beth Balbierz
Diagrams by Lori Enik

Library of Congress Cataloging-in-Publication Data
Crisfield, Deborah.
  Knack coaching youth soccer : step-by-step instruction
on strategy, mechanics, drills, and winning / D.W. Crisfield ;
photographs by Beth Balbierz.
     p. cm.
  Includes index.
  ISBN 978-1-59921-548-8
  1. Soccer for children--Coaching. I. Balbierz, Beth, ill. II. Title.
  GV944.2.C75 2009
  796.334083--dc22
                    2009010783

The following manufacturers/names appearing in Knack
Coaching Youth Soccer are trademarks:
ACE®, Gatorade®, Nike®, Ping-Pong®, Velcro®, VSport™, YouTube™

Printed in China

10 9 8 7 6 5 4 3 2 1

To all the great youth soccer players who posed for the photos in this book.

Acknowledgments

First and foremost, I have to thank Laura Madden for her extensive knowledge, the hours she spent filling in the blanks and creating photo shoots, and her attention to detail. The book would not have been possible without her support. Beth Balbierz was also vital to the top-notch quality of this book. I'm very appreciative of her fabulous photography and her ability to interpret my instructions and capture some wonderful soccer moments. I'd also like to thank Dave Ophel, a fabulous co-coach, for sticking with me through eighteen seasons of soccer; Alex Feltes, a terrific goalkeeper, for always being available to answer my questions; Katie Benoit for seeing this book through to production; Maureen Graney for taking a chance on an author she doesn't know; and Gary Krebs for still having my name in his writer files. And finally I'd like to thank Tony and Bobby for their companionship and constant source of entertainment during the writing of this book.

For Rob, Samantha, & Derek

Photographer Acknowledgments

First of all, I would like to thank my family (including Mom, Dad, and Amy) because without them and their support, I would not have been able to complete this book. To my daughter Samantha, who was so patient and understanding when she was a part of so many photo shoots. I also want to thank all of the players, coaches, and parents from the Jersey Knights Cavalry, Franklin Avengers, Franklin Flames, the Summit Travel, and Recreation teams, and those in Connecticut who let me photograph them. Without you, I would not have been able to illustrate Debbie's words. Thank you to Jon Naso of The Record for suggesting I do the photography for this book. Finally, I want to thank Debbie Crisfield, Laura Madden, Maureen Graney, and Katie Benoit for their time and energy in working with me.

The *Knack Coaching Youth Soccer* team would also like to thank Peter Chapman and six2six soccer, a Connecticut-based organization that raises money for local charities, for allowing us to photograph the organization's annual soccer marathon for the pages of this book.

CONTENTS

INTRODUCTION

If you've picked up this book, you're most likely considering volunteering your time as a youth coach. Maybe you're testing the waters before agreeing to it, or perhaps you've already been roped in. Maybe you already have a season under your belt, but those two or three months convinced you that you need more resources. No matter what your motivation for choosing this book, I hope you find in it the necessary instruction, philosophy, and inspiration to turn a simple volunteer activity into a rewarding and long-lasting experience.

For me, coaching youth soccer has been one of the most worthwhile and gratifying opportunities I've had during my life. I've coached players as young as five and as old as sixteen. I've coached in-town teams, travel teams, and one high school team. I've coached my own children and their friends, and I've also coached teams full of complete strangers. I've coached boys' teams, girls' teams, and co-ed teams. I've coached by myself and with co-coaches.

Even though my job was to impart the skills, the strategies, and the joys of the game of soccer to these young players, I found that each team and each season was also providing valuable instruction to me. The fourteen-year-old girls I'm coaching now have certainly reaped the benefits of my twenty-one years of coaching experience, whereas those twelve-year-old boys who were my first guinea pigs could probably use a redo. They deserved better, but they got the best I had at the time. I should have grabbed a book like this before I went out onto the field because I expected to coach as if I were coaching a college team, and they expected to have fun. That was the first and best lesson I've learned along the way.

Although I've had two undefeated teams and a dramatic shoot-out loss in the championship finals, some of my favorite seasons have been those when the team didn't do so well. Some seasons and some teams have been better than others, and the win-loss record had nothing to do with it. When I was coaching my son's first-grade team—the Bluegrass Ghosts—we didn't win a single game, and we scored a grand total of two goals all season, but the team was filled with a bunch of smiling, happy cutie pies who didn't care one bit, so I count that as one of my favorite seasons.

The core players of my current team—a U-14 girls team that includes my daughter and quite a few of her friends—have been with me since they began in the local in-town league as kindergarteners. Over the years we've added players and lost others, but we've always been the Summit Charge, and the chemistry on the team has remained largely the same. They're a bunch of fun, positive, motivated girls who generally listen, generally try hard, and are a complete joy to be around. Spring of 2009 will be my last season with them and probably my last season as a soccer coach. I'll be ending on a great note.

This book is a comprehensive youth soccer coaching guide. It should be valuable not only for the novice coach, eager to learn the ropes, but also for the experienced coach who wants to add to his reservoir of knowl-

edge and supplement his practices with new, fun, and productive drills and games.

Youth soccer is a broad term that encompasses a huge variety of philosophies and leagues. This book tries to give a balanced view that doesn't favor one over the other, and it covers strategies to help you find the league that is right for your coaching style. Of course, many volunteer coaches find themselves in this position because they're following their children. In that case, you may not be able to pick and choose your team. But certain coach-

Quite often in the book, I've divided the information into three age groups: the 4- to 6-year-olds, the 7- to 10-year-olds, and the 11- to 14-year-olds. These are natural breaks in most youth soccer leagues, and obviously you would not treat or teach a four year old the same way you would a fourteen-year-old.

Much of the book targets specific soccer skills: dribbling, passing, ball control, shooting, heading, and goalkeeping. The mechanics of each are broken down into basic steps that make it easy for both the coach and player to understand. In addition, I've included games and drills to help cement these skills into the players' minds and muscle memory.

ing styles are better suited to certain leagues. Finding the right fit will help make your experience enjoyable.

The book also covers practical matters, such as rules and equipment and training the soccer body. These chapters are probably more helpful for the new coach than to the experienced coach, but it's a nice resource for everyone. The age of your players will also dictate whether parts of this book are useful. For example, stretching, strength training, and endurance training will all help any team improve, but the age level and intensity level of your players will dictate how much of this will be part of your practice routine.

Games are a great way to learn. They make practices fun and enjoyable learning experiences. I've mentioned the fun factor already in this introduction, and I'll repeat it several times in this book because it can't be emphasized enough. Kids play sports for fun, so a large part of your job as the coach is to make sure that they're having fun.

The second half of the book moves into strategy, with chapters on set plays, formations, defense, offense, and transition. Most of the information found in these chapters will be valuable for coaches of older players. Tactics and strategies are wasted on the youngest players, but if you're a coach who is new to the sport, the information found in these chapters will give you a better understanding of the game of soccer.

Most coaches think that most of their work is done in practices, and although that's largely true, games and tryouts come with their own coaching issues—not to mention parent interaction. I've addressed a few of these issues to make those extra moments work for you.

I hope you find both this book and your coaching experience rewarding. I initially became a coach because I felt it was important to give something to my community, but the upside of being around kids who are having fun has made me think that perhaps my selfless volunteering has turned into pure selfishness. If you're a coach in the beginning stages, wondering if this is going to be a good fit, I urge you to give it a try. Read this book, focus on fun, and stick it out for more than one season. The more prepared you are and the more fun you have, the more both you and the kids will enjoy the experience.

YOUR COACHING PERSONALITY

Winning isn't everything . . . or is it? Find your coaching style

Every coach has a different style, and for most that style is not a conscious decision. At one extreme we have the highly competitive coaches, out to win at all costs regardless of the egos being trampled on the field. At the other extreme we have the cheerleaders, with all the focus on making the experience positive and fun but pushing the idea of both learning and winning to the back burner.

The best coaches find a balance between the two extremes.

You have stepped into the position of coach for a reason. You are there to teach a group of children the rules, the skills, the thrills, and the pure enjoyment of playing soccer. It's imperative that you keep all of those in mind for every practice and game.

Although your personality is pretty ingrained by the time you've reached the coaching stage, you do need to tailor your style to suit both the age of your players and the league

The Whistle

- The quintessential picture of a coach always shows an adult with a whistle around his neck, but many coaches prefer to use their voices.

- Whistles come in handy during an in-practice scrimmage. Tell your players to

freeze when they hear a whistle, and it will give you an opportunity to point out a positioning problem.

- Try not to blow the whistle too often because doing so can disrupt the flow of the game.

Pinnies

- Pinnies are loose mesh vests that players can slip on over their shirts to give the illusion of a uniform, thereby clarifying who is on which team.

- Pinnies can also be used on the field to mark goals or boundaries.

- Some pinnies are reversible, allowing for two different colors. If your budget is unlimited, getting one for every person on the team is ideal.

- Aside from the uses in practice, pinnies can be especially handy if you find yourself playing a game against a team of the same color.

that your team plays in. Some leagues insist on noncompetitive, learning-based programs. Some are more competitive but require equal playing time and full inclusion. Others are focused on development and winning, holding tryouts to create elite teams with highly skilled players. If you know your coaching personality up front, then you should do your best to choose a league to match your style.

YELLOW LIGHT

No matter what your philosophy is, in order to teach effectively, you're going to need to grab your players' attention. These kids are used to fast-paced video games, eight hundred TV channels with remote controls, limitless websites, and YouTube videos. Their minds and their attention spans have been trained to expect information to come in quick and entertaining bursts. The long lecture won't work here.

Cones and Disks

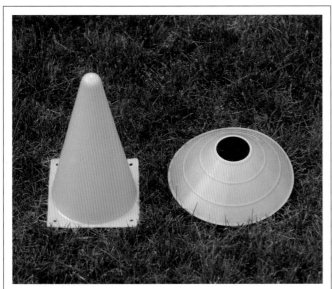

- Cones and disks are used in an enormous amount of drills, so they're a coach's handy tool as well.

- They can mark boundaries or smaller goals.

- Cones have the added advantage of being able to be knocked over, an advantage that can be incorporated into some drills.

- Some coaches prefer to buy actual small goals, but if that's not in your budget, the cones, disks, and pinnies do an excellent job of delineating a goal as well.

Clipboard

- Soccer is mostly an outdoor game, so if you have a practice plan, it's nice to be able to clip it to a windproof board.

- Part of coaching necessarily involves paperwork, so having a clipboard to keep it all in order can be helpful. In addition to practice plans, coaches usually need to have rosters, notes on players, and emergency contacts.

- A "dry erase" clipboard can also be used to illustrate set plays or formations.

PHILOSOPHY TO SUIT THE AGES

As players age, practices change, but they should always focus on fun

The beauty of soccer is that it's such a simple game that even four-year-olds can begin having fun with it. They might not grasp the big picture, but they get the idea that they're supposed to use their feet, they're supposed to get the ball into the goal, and they have a couple of other people helping them and a couple of people trying to stop them from doing it. That's definitely something a four-year-old can handle.

The other marvelous thing about soccer is that it is a nuanced game in which layers upon layers of sophistication and skill can be added as the players get older. Because soccer can be played at all these different levels, coaches need to modify their approach depending on the age of their

The Youngest Age Group

- When a child starts playing soccer at age four or five, he certainly doesn't yet have a passion for the game. In fact, most children won't even know what the game is. Your only goal now is to create an environment in which the kids are having fun.

- Keep your practices silly. Play lots of games and make the kids hungry for more.

- Be sure they know the basic rules of the game—the object is to get the ball in the net—but don't worry about explaining much more.

- Play time during games should be equal for all.

Seven to Ten Years

- Focus on positive reinforcement. Point out when a child does something great.

- Keep criticism to a minimum.

- Introduce the finer points of both rules and skills, but don't take away the fun. Most of the skills can be practiced using fun games.

- This age is the time to start teaching positions, but be sure you don't pigeonhole a player into a position.

- Play time should continue to be equal for all. You never know who might emerge as a great player all of a sudden.

players. Regardless of the age, however, coaches should re-member that the kids are there for an enjoyable experience. Youth soccer should not be treated as a college sport just with younger players. Keep it fun. Keep it positive.

Finally, because you've stepped up to coach, chances are you love sports and competition, but as much as we all like to win, you have to always remember that as a coach you are first and foremost a role model for these kids. They need to learn how to win and lose with grace as much as they need to learn how to play the game.

Older Players

- By the time kids reach the oldest level of youth soccer, they are looking for some real instruction.

- Practices should focus more on higher-level concepts rather than on basic skills.

- Players should really start focusing on one or two posi-tions. Whole-team strategy can develop at this age.

- Playing time does not need to be equally distributed. Although everyone should get some playing time (and leagues usually have guide-lines for this), the players are transitioning to scholastic play where the goal is to win.

GREEN ● LIGHT

As the kids age, they should also learn to be more inde-pendent on the field. They should know who takes the corner kicks, who takes the goal kicks, and so forth. The coach shouldn't have to be yelling instructions from the sideline. As you allow the kids to become more indepen-dent, natural team leaders will emerge as well.

Ideas for All

- Keep it fun.

- Try to have a focus.

- Introduce variety by mixing individual and group games and drills.

- Include a scrimmage in every practice.

- End on a positive note.

3

TRAVEL, REC, INDOOR, CAMP
Soccer styles to suit every player: indoor and outdoor, preschool to preteen

Youth soccer comes in all different shapes and sizes, from clinics for three-years-olds to elite teams that travel to other states playing tournaments. In some towns, soccer is a one-season sport, and in others it's an year-around sport.

If you've picked up this book, you've probably already been pressed into a coaching job, so you're most likely not in a position to pick and choose which type of youth soccer you'll participate in. But on the off chance that you still are unsure which direction to follow, there are four main opportunities for coaching: travel soccer, rec soccer, camp or clinic soccer, and indoor soccer.

Encourage your kids to go to camp. They can go to camps

Travel Soccer

- As the term implies, travel soccer involves teams that travel to other towns to play.

- These teams tend to be highly regulated, requiring official rosters and cards at every match.

- The leagues here vary. Some are elite, have tryouts, and focus on winning, whereas some are all-inclusive and have strict rules of equal playing time, emphasizing participation over wins. Most are somewhere in between.

- After the players reach about ten years old, most teams have moved to a more competitive focus.

Rec Soccer

- Recreation soccer is usually played in an in-town league. Every town will have its own rules, but usually these leagues emphasize participation and fun and are not overly competitive.

- Typically, the uniforms are T-shirts—different colors all bearing the same town logo, sometimes with sponsors from local businesses.

- Most teams for children under age eight play this type of soccer. In many leagues the teams are not supposed to keep score.

4

as individuals, or, if you're lucky, you can get your whole team to go together. Some are day camps, and some are sleep-away camps. Usually you sign up for a week at a time. You can also have your players sign up for clinics. These would focus on specific skills, such as a shooting clinic for forwards. Clinics tend to be once a week over an extended period of time.

Even if your focus is outdoor soccer, you can bring your team indoors during the off season. Indoor soccer is a faster game, which gives players more touches on the ball. It's a great way for them to both maintain and improve their skills.

····· YELLOW ●LIGHT ·····

The quality of soccer camps varies. Get a recommendation before you commit your child to long camp hours.

Indoor Soccer

- Indoor soccer uses most of the skills and rules of regular soccer, but it does have a few quirks of its own that are discussed in Chapter 19.

- Usually a coach ends up in an indoor league because he wants to extend the autumn season and give his players more time on the ball.

- If you don't have a team and are looking to do some coaching, you may want to contact an indoor facility to see if it needs assistance.

Soccer Camps

- During the summer there's an explosion of soccer camps. These can range from fun activities for young children to serious training for players who are interested in taking their soccer to the next level.

- A camp for young children should focus on fun and a variety of activities.

- A rigorous camp for older children probably includes four or five sessions of soccer a day.

MEETING YOUR TEAM
You're a leader, a teacher, an entertainer, and a role model

First impressions are everything. When you meet your team for the first time, what image do you want to convey? What messages do you want to give the kids? Plan your introduction as much as you plan your practices. You get one chance to make a first impression. This applies to your practice, too. Craft a really fun practice for the first time out. Most importantly, make sure you end with something fun so they leaave feeling they've had a great time.

For the youngest children, you're going to want to keep talk to a minimum. Be warm and enthusiastic and get them moving quickly. You might be coaching children who are still dealing with some separation anxiety, so it's best if you don't give them much time to think about it. Tell them your name and then get them moving around the field. As they're moving, you can jog around with them and try to learn their names.

Good Rules for All Ages

- Have mutual respect.
- Don't talk when the coach is talking.
- Support teammates.
- Try your hardest.
- Keep it fun.

Four- to Six-year-olds

- The four- to six-year-olds who are photographed in this book are from a co-ed rec league. This particular rec league is sponsored by the YMCA, but many rec leagues are sponsored by a town.

- The teams do not travel to other towns. They play each other.

- Typically, a practice will be on the same day as the game, usually no more than thirty minutes and right before the game.

- No score is kept.

The older the children are, the more instructions you can give them, but it's never a good idea to talk for a long time. In your introductions, you want to make your expectations clear but don't overwhelm the players with too many things at once. You want your instructions to stick.

ZOOM

Balls come in different sizes depending on the ages for both health and satisfaction reasons.

four- to six-year-olds	size 3
seven- to ten-year-olds	size 4
eleven- to fourteen-year-olds	size 5
high school	size 5
college	size 5
professional	size 5

Seven- to Ten-year-olds

- The seven- to ten-year-olds in this book are from two teams.

- The girls are on a U-9 team called "Summit Freedom," and they play in a travel league in central and northern New Jersey.

- The boys are also on a U-9 travel team called the "Franklin Avengers" in central New Jersey.

Eleven- to Fourteen-year-olds

- The older kids photographed for this book are from three U-14 girls teams.

- One is a select travel team called the "Jersey Knights Cavalry." This team draws elite players from several surrounding towns.

- The other two teams are from Summit, N.J. The Summit Speedways are a competitive travel team, and the Summit Charge are in a recreational league, although it also plays against other towns.

MEETING THE PARENTS
Parents can be valuable assets, so keep them in the loop

Your players are somebody's children first and soccer players second. Learn how to play to all your audiences. Today's parents are much more involved in their children's lives, schools, and activities than they ever have been. You may be expecting to re-create your experience as a player, remembering that it was just the team and the coach with no parents in sight. Many of today's parents want to be much more involved—almost a third aspect of the team experience.

If this is going to be difficult for you, you should go on the offensive. Create opportunities for parents to be involved before they jump in and dictate the options to you. If there's any aspect of coaching that you don't like, give it to them. Ask for people to organize halftime beverages or snacks. See if someone wants to be in charge of finding and e-mailing directions to away games. Someone else can be in charge of an end-of-season party.

Parent Meeting

- Some coaches like to have a face-to-face meeting before the start of the season just to set the tone. Others prefer to do this through e-mail.

- You'll want to address your philosophy on playing time and expectations for attendance.

- Stress the importance of communication.

- If players aren't happy with something, parents should feel comfortable coming to you.

Sportsmanship

- When you meet with the parents, tell them that your goal is to be a good role model for the players and that you expect the same of them.

- Encourage parents to cheer when there's a good play but not to instruct from the sideline.

- One fun way for parents to show their support is to make a bridge at the end of the game. The parents stand across from each other and execute double high fives as the team members run under the bridge.

Finally, most parents appreciate organization and good communication. Be sure you have everyone's e-mail address and be sure to update them as much as possible. Make it clear to parents that they need to communicate with you as well if their child is going to miss a game or practice.

Halftime Snacks

- Some teams require that each player bring a water bottle to the game. Other teams like something more elaborate.

- The most popular halftime snack is oranges. Please encourage parents to cut them. An easier fruit would be grapes.

- Find a parent volunteer to organize the halftime snack schedule.

- On synthetic turf fields, parents are going to be limited to what they can bring. Most fields prohibit food and sugary drinks.

Homework

- There are many drills that a player can do at home, from juggling in the backyard to practicing dribbling moves to using a ball on a rope.

- Tell parents to compare soccer to school or piano lessons. Kids have to practice in between.

- Today's kids are highly programmed and overscheduled, so finding free time to practice might be a factor. But the one thing that hasn't changed is that kids won't instantly be talented. Soccer is a skill that needs to be worked on.

GETTING TO KNOW YOUR TEAM
Learn who your players are as they get to know each other, too

Some people are good with names, and some are not. It's just a fact of life. Nonetheless, you have to make it a priority to learn your players' names as fast as possible. They know your name immediately, and especially the youngest ones won't grasp why you might not know their names.

Study your list of names before you go to practice. That will at least give you a base. A number of name games are listed on this page. Not only will they let the children get to know each other, but also they will help you to learn the children's names under the guise of letting them get to know each other.

Some teams like to foster team unity with activities outside of practices or games. This isn't really necessary with the youngest players, but it can be a nice addition to older teams. Try a team picnic or a parent/child game. If you have a college or a professional soccer franchise near you, take the

Focus Points for a Coach

• Learn who your speedsters are.

• Make a note of the aggressive players.

• Discover your team leaders.

• Learn how to neutralize your team troublemakers.

• Start to figure out who is most effective at each position.

Greetings

• Soccer is a team game, so players need to be comfortable and friendly with each other. This drill will help foster both.

• All the players should be running around randomly inside the box. The coach yells out a greeting, which the players then must execute: high five, low five, shake hands, fist bump.

• Tell the players they have to greet a different person each time.

team to a game. This is certainly not necessary, but it will create team bonding and a sense of camaraderie. Off-the-field connections can sometimes translate into tighter unity on the field.

The Name Circle

- This fun game helps kids learn each other's names.

- Sit in a circle holding a ball. Begin by saying, "My name is Coach _____." Then pass the ball to the next player.

- That player must say his name and yours, then pass the ball on. The next player says his name, the previous player's name, and yours. This process continues around the circle as the list gets longer.

- When the ball makes its way back to you, you have to repeat every single name in the circle.

Calling for a Pass

- This drill is played on half a field. Give a ball to everyone except three players.

- Players should dribble around the field. The three players without a ball have to call to someone with a ball, using his or her name.

- This game teaches kids to talk on the field.

- Expand the game for older children by including their location. For example, "Teddy, I'm open on the sideline," or "Alex, pass it back."

11

OBJECT OF THE GAME
Know the rules of soccer before you start coaching

Soccer unquestionably is the most popular game worldwide. Estimates put the number of official players at roughly a quarter-billion. And that doesn't include all those empty-lot, street-playing, pickup game soccer fans who play whenever they can find an open space. So what makes soccer so popular? It could be that the game is both simple enough for a small child to understand and intricate enough to be incredibly challenging.

On the face of it, soccer is a pretty simple game. Two teams. One ball. Don't use your hands, and try to get that ball into the opponent's goal. Simple, right? On the surface, it really is, and that's the part of soccer that makes it a game that can be fun even for four-year-olds.

On the flip side, the Federation Internationale de Football Association (FIFA), which is the governing body of soccer worldwide, has a full book outlining the rules of soccer. And

Goal of the Game

- Soccer is played with two teams, two goals, and one ball.

- The object of soccer is to get the ball into the opponent's goal.

- The ball may be moved backward, forward, and sideways by any number of players, as long as the field players do not touch the ball with any part of their arms or hands.

- The game is played in two forty-five-minute halves. The time is running time and is not stopped for free kicks, out of bounds, goals, or substitutions.

The Actual Goal

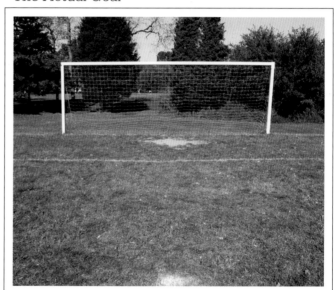

- Official goals are 8 feet high and 24 feet wide. The crossbar and the two posts must be white; they must all be the same width, which must not exceed 5 inches.

- The goals are placed so the front of the goalpost is on the inner part of the end line.

- The ball must fully cross the end line to be considered a goal.

- Each team is allowed one player, the goalkeeper, who can touch the ball with his hands.

this book includes many more rules than the ones included in the short paragraph above. In fact, there are 133 pages of rules.

As a coach, you need to learn as many of the rules as you can, but the field, the number of players, the length of the game, and the goal dimensions will vary depending on the age of your team. Young players might even use cones for their goals, and they probably won't even keep score. Your league should make these factors clear up front.

Moving the Ball

- There are eleven players on each team: ten field players and one goalkeeper.

- The players have several options for moving the ball down the field. They can move it by themselves,

which is called "dribbling," or they can use a series of passes.

- Older kids may also use their heads to direct an air ball in one direction or another.

Rough Play

- Although rules regulate physical contact on the field, it is allowed. Players may use their bodies to jockey for position.

- Players may not push, trip, hold, or intentionally

rough up another player. If a player does any of these actions, he'll be called for a foul.

- Egregious fouls may result in expulsion from the game.

PLAYING FIELD

Lines, circles, boxes, arcs, and hash marks tell you where to go

The dimensions of a soccer field may vary, but at the outer limits the field can be enormous: 100 yards wide and 130 yards long. That's bigger than the field of just about any other sport (except for the potentially limitless women's lacrosse). The regulation soccer field must be a rectangle, and it must be between 100 and 130 yards long and 50 and 100 yards wide. The lines at the two ends of the field are called the "goal lines" or "end lines." The lines connecting them are called the

"sidelines" or "touchlines." The length of the touchline must always be greater than the length of the goal line.

Some fields will be in much better condition than others. Some will have beautifully manicured green grass, some will be synthetic turf, and some will be hard-packed dirt disasters. Some might be a combination of a soccer field and baseball infield, so your players will have to cope with different surfaces in one field.

Using the Lines

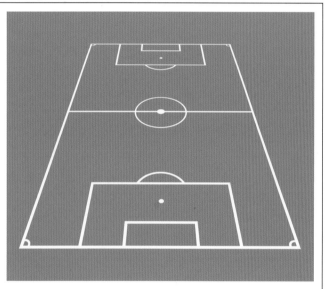

- If the ball goes over the sideline, it is returned to play with a throw. If the ball goes over the end line, it is returned to play with a kick.

- A line cuts across the center of the field, dividing it in half widthwise. A 10-yard circle surrounds the exact center of this line.

- A hash mark is 12 yards out and directly in the center of the goal. At the top of the 18-yard box, a portion of a circle marks the area 10 yards away from the hash mark.

The Positions

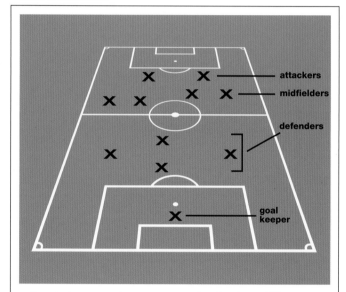

attackers
midfielders
defenders
goal keeper

- Regulation soccer has eleven players on the field.

- These players are generally divided into three groups: attackers, midfielders, defenders, and one goal-keeper (who is considered part of the defense).

- Coaches have different formations, but almost all use these four positions in some variation.

- A team is not required to have a goalkeeper, although not having one would be very unusual.

Before each game, it is good for a coach to walk the field. You may want to remove stray rocks. Coaches may file a formal complaint or suggest to the referee that the game be forfeited if they feel strongly that the field is unsafe.

The conditions of the field may also affect your coaching decisions. Notice if the field has a slope, if one goal mouth is more damaged, or if the sun is shining at an angle that would affect a keeper's goal-saving ability.

The Goal Boxes

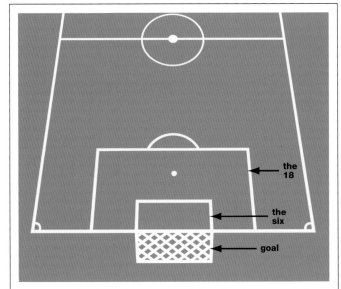

- In front of each goal are two boxes. One is 6 yards out from the goal in all directions. People refer to this as "the 6."

- Goal kicks must be taken from within the 6-yard box.

- The other box is 18 yards out in all directions and is referred to as "the 18."

- The 18-yard box is the area in which goalkeepers can use their hands. In addition, if a foul is committed within this box, then a penalty kick rather than a direct kick is awarded.

Offsides

The other team's goalkeeper may count as one of the defenders.

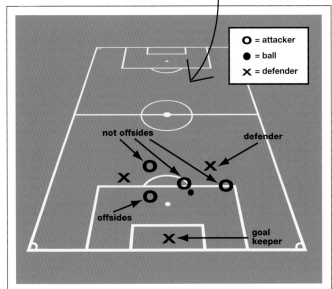

- A player needs to keep either the ball or two defenders between him and the goal at all times or else he will be called "offsides."

- Complicating this rule are the exceptions. If a player is on his own half of the field he can't be offsides.

- A player cannot be offsides if he receives the ball directly from a throw-in, goal kick, or corner kick.

- Also, if a player is never involved in the play, he is not offsides. He is offsides only if the ball gets passed to him.

THROW-INS

Teach your players how to inbound the ball from the sidelines with their hands

The throw-in is used when the ball goes out of bounds over the sideline. Because soccer is a game played primarily with the feet, this way of inbounding the ball has always struck me as odd. If the ball goes over the end line, it's returned to play with a kick. Why not the sidelines, too? In addition, the rules behind the throw require some of the most restricted throw-ing movements in sports—perhaps to emphasize how unwelcome the use of hands actually is in this game of "football." Both feet must be on the ground, the ball must be thrown with two hands, and the ball must go entirely over the head.

If a player does not execute the throw-in properly, then the ball is turned over to the other team for a throw-in.

Feet on the Ground

- When a player releases the ball, both feet must be touching the ground.

- A player may choose, however, whether or not to stand square or have one foot in front of the other.

- This is the hardest part of the technique for the youngest players and generally will not be strictly enforced for quite some time.

Dragging the Foot

- Players can take a running start to boost the power behind the throw.

- Have your players take a few steps and then, when they release the ball, drag the top of their back foot along the ground.

- Some players try to gain extra distance by doing a flip first. They grasp the ball with two hands, take a running start, plant the ball on the ground, and flip over. When they land on their feet, they release the ball. The momentum of the flip sends the ball farther.

A few other rules pertain to throw-ins: The player who throws the ball in may not touch it until another player—from either team—touches it first. No one can be offsides. The strategy behind throw-ins depends on the players' ages and abilities. Younger players should throw the ball down at the feet of their teammates. Older players should get some distance. If the players are in front of their own goal, they should throw the ball down the sideline, keeping it away from the middle of the field, unless someone is obviously open. If they're in front of the opponent's goal, then they should toss the ball into the center.

The Release

- The player must use both hands to make the throw.

- He should grip the ball firmly and be sure both hands remain on the ball for the entire throw.

- The rules require that the throw begin behind the head.

- The ball must then pass straight over the head before it is released.

Two Hands

- The release must come from both hands at the same time.

- The referees will look for any spin on the ball, which would indicate that one hand was more dominant than the other.

- A player can make a long,

lofted throw or a shorter throw to an open teammate's foot.

- Players need to move to get open. They also should know the thrower's strength. There's no point in standing 30 feet away when the thrower can't throw that far.

SPECIAL KICKS
Corner kicks, goal kicks, direct kicks, indirect kicks, and penalty kicks galore

Play is stopped for a variety of reasons. It's stopped when the ball goes out of bounds, when a player has committed a foul, when there's an injury on the field, or when a goal has been scored. For each of these instances, play is restarted in a different fashion.

A play for most of these kicks (not the penalty kick) can be restarted in a slow manner or a fast manner. The player doesn't have to wait for a whistle from the referee. If the kicker feels that her team would have an advantage if she kicked the ball quickly before the other team set up, she may do that. On the other hand, she might want to give her team a chance to get in place or move down the field.

KNACK COACHING YOUTH SOCCER

Kickoff

Although it's highly unlikely, a goal may be scored directly from a kickoff.

- Every game begins with a kickoff. The ball is placed on the center of the midfield line. Both teams must have all eleven players on their own side of the field.

- The defending team must be entirely out of the center circle.

- The kickoff begins when the ball moves forward. The player who moved the ball first may not touch the ball again until someone else has touched it.

- Kickoffs are also used to resume play after a goal is scored, to start the second half, or to start overtime.

Penalty Kick

- A penalty kick is a one-on-one kick awarded to a team when the defenders have committed a foul within the penalty box.

- The goalkeeper for the defending team is the only player allowed in front of the goal. The attacking team is allowed one shoot-er. All other players must be outside the boundaries of the penalty box.

- The ball is placed on the hash mark, which is 12 yards away from the goal.

- The keeper must have both feet on the goal line until the ball is kicked.

Some defenses try to delay the kicker by moving in closer than the required 10 yards. The kicker will then have to ask the referee to move these players back. Doing this prevents the kicker from making the quick kick. If the kicker asks the referee to move the players back, then he must wait for a whistle before he kicks the ball. One additional note: The coach is not able to ask for the 10 yards. It must be asked for by the player taking the kick.

Goal Kick

- A goal kick is awarded when the attacking team kicks the ball over the end line.

- The ball must be placed within the goal box—the 6-yard line.

- The ball must leave the penalty box to be in play.

The kicker may not touch the ball again until someone else has touched it.

- If the kicker does touch the ball again, the other team gets an indirect kick. If a player touches the ball before it leaves the box, the kick is retaken.

Corner Kick

- A corner kick is taken when the defending team kicks the ball over the goal line. A goal may be scored directly from a corner kick.

- In the corner of the field is a quarter circle 1 yard out from the goal line to the touch line. The attacking

team places the ball anywhere within this arc.

- Defenders must stand at least 10 yards away.

- The corner kicker may not touch the ball again until it has been touched by another player.

REFEREE SIGNALS

Know what the referee means when he blows his whistle

Every soccer game should have at least one referee, although at the youngest levels this referee might be the coach, too. As the competition grows, the quality and number of referees also increase.

Teams at a younger age tend to have less-experienced referees. Also, depending on the league rules, these referees might not even be certified. Coaches should make it clear to their players' parents that these referees are also learning along with the children. Mistakes are more likely to happen, and no one should get upset with the referees.

When there is only one referee, each team provides a linesman. The referee officiates in the center of the field, and the two linesmen run up and down the sidelines to indicate when the ball has gone out of bounds. These linesmen may not be the coach, and they may make only the out-of-bounds calls.

As competition increases, games might have two or three

KNACK COACHING YOUTH SOCCER

Direct Kicks

- A direct kick is a free kick awarded to a team after the other team has fouled it. This kick is taken at the point of the foul and may go directly into the goal on the kick.

- The referee will signal a direct kick by pointing with a raised arm toward the goal of the offending team.

- The following fouls are considered serious enough to warrant a direct kick: kicking, tripping, charging, pushing, tackling, holding, spitting at a player, or making a handball.

Indirect Kicks

- The indirect kick is taken at the point of the infraction; the ball must touch one other player (on either team) before it goes into the goal.

- The referee signals this kick by keeping his hand above his head.

- If the foul is inside the penalty box, the kick is taken on the 18, nearest to the foul.

- These kicks are awarded for dangerous play (such as kicking the ball while he is on the ground or lifting his foot near someone else's head); if a player is offsides; and if a player gets in the way of an opponent.

officials. If the game has two officials, one of them takes one sideline and one end line, and the other takes the remaining two lines. If the game has three officials, two of the referees will be linesmen, but they are able to make calls such as offsides or a handball in the box.

More Complicated Offsides Rules

- The offsides rule presents an extra challenge for a referee.

- It is legal for a player to step out of bounds to confirm that he has no intention of being involved in the play (during which he cannot be offsides).

- However, if a defender steps out of bounds in order to remove himself from the field of play and thereby makes an attacker offsides because he doesn't have two defenders between him and the goal, then the defender will get a yellow card.

The Ref's Whistle

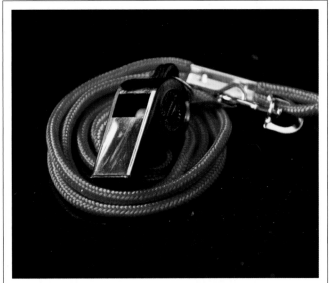

- Referees blow their whistle to start the game.

- After a ball goes out of bounds or a free kick is awarded, the team in possession of the ball may inbound it or kick it without waiting for a whistle.

- Referees don't need to blow their whistle when the ball goes out of bounds.

- Most often, referees blow their whistles to stop play. They stop play when a foul has been committed; when a goal has been scored; when a half has ended; and when an injury has occurred.

21

EXTRA RULES
You need to know about quirky aspects of soccer

Although soccer can be a highly physical game, safeguards are in place to preserve the ideals of sportsmanship. Players are expected to treat each other and the referee with respect. They are not allowed to do anything that might give them an advantage, such as preventing a goal with the hands if they are not a goalkeeper. Players can't even try to fake out the other team by calling for the ball—that is poor sportsmanship.

If a player shows poor sportsmanship on the field, the referee might give him or her a yellow card. A yellow card is a warning that a player is not playing within the spirit of the game. If a player gets two yellow cards in a game, he is given a red card. The red card means that the player is removed from the game, and he may not be replaced. The team must play short one player. Many leagues require the player to sit out the next game.

Drop Kicks

- A drop kick is taken when the referee is unable to award the ball to either team. This situation happens when the referee stops play for an injury or a disturbance on the field.

- One player from each team is involved in the drop kick.

- The referee drops the ball in the exact spot where play was stopped. Players may not kick the ball until it touches the ground.

- If play stops in the goal area, the drop kick takes place on the 18 nearest to the spot where play was stopped.

Overtime and Shootouts

- In soccer, low scoring is the norm, so often a game ends in a tie. Most leagues end the game at this point and record the score as a tie.

- Some leagues play two short overtime periods. Some leagues make the overtime "sudden death,"

- which means the first team to score is the winner.

- Others use a shootout, taking penalty kicks until there is a winner.

- Some leagues play overtime first, then use a shootout as a last resort.

Yellow cards and red cards are given in other circumstances as well, although they are given only for serious or semiserious infractions. Normal fouls do not bring out the cards.

Indirect kicks are also awarded for the following goalkeeper offenses: (1) If the keeper takes more than six seconds to release the ball. (2) If the keeper releases the ball and then touches it with his hands again before it has touched another player. (3) If the keeper catches a throw-in from his own teammate.

ZOOM

Yellow Card Infractions: Engaging in unsportsmanlike behavior, having a voiced disagreement with the referee, wasting time, refusing to stay 10 yards away from a kick, moving on or off the field without permission

Red Card Infractions: Committing a serious, dangerous foul, being violent, spitting, blocking a goal with the hands by a nongoalkeeper (also an automatic goal), using bad language

Subbing

- Sub rules vary dramatically depending on age. At the youngest levels, there may be no sub rules. You may not even have to notify the referee that you're subbing.

- Official FIFA rules for international matches allow for only three substitutions in an entire match.

- Most leagues are somewhere in between these two extremes, some limiting subs only to when a throw-in is done or when the subbing team has the ball.

- The referee must acknowledge the subs before they come in.

Passing to the Keeper

- If a player passes the ball back to the team's goalkeeper, the keeper may not use his hands and instead must kick the ball just like any other field player.

- However, if the pass back is with the head, or if a ball ricochets off a teammate and is not a deliberate pass back, then the keeper may use his hands.

- If the keeper touches the ball with his hands when he was not supposed to, the opposing team will get an indirect kick on the 18.

SAFETY FIRST

A coach needs to keep players' safety uppermost in mind

Soccer is a contact sport. Players get hurt on a regular basis, but leagues, coaches, and referees all need to take many precautions to minimize injuries.

Coaches can be prepared with first aid kits, plenty of fluids, and a basic knowledge of first aid. They also should take care not to push an injured player to continue to play if she suffers any sort of injury. She should be immediately taken off the field in order to be assessed. Some injuries might hurt in the moment but not require attention, but others might be exacerbated or even dangerous if the player is allowed to continue to play.

A referee's job is to stop play when he recognizes that an injury has occurred. If the referee deems that the player is only slightly injured, he allows play to continue until a natural stoppage occurs. If, however, the referee deems the player to be seriously injured, he blows the whistle to stop play for

First Aid Kit

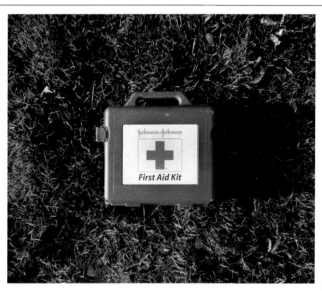

- Every coach should have a first aid kit at every practice and game.

- Although most injuries are not serious, all of them can benefit from immediate treatment.

- First aid kits should include ice packs, adhesive bandages, ACE bandages, antibiotic ointment, gauze and tape, scissors, and plastic gloves.

Ice Packs

- If a child gets an injury that does not involve a cut or an abrasion, the most likely treatment will be an ice pack.

- Ice packs are good for sprains, strains, pulled muscles, and concussions.

- In an injury, blood rushes to the area, causing swelling. Ice constricts the blood vessels, so putting an ice pack on the injured area reduces the blood flow and therefore reduces the swelling.

- Because ice packs are key for early intervention, be sure to check on your supply regularly.

the injury. His first obligation is to remove the injured player from the field so the player can receive treatment. Treatment should not be given on the field. Coaches should instruct their team members to sit down on the field or go down onto one knee when another player is injured, whether on their team or the opponents' team.

If play has been stopped for an injury, the referee will usually restart play with a dropped ball. He will also add time on the clock to replace the amount of time taken up by the removal of the player from the field.

And at all times (although especially in hot weather), coaches should be sure there is plenty of water available and allow for water breaks during practice. Heat cramps, heat exhaustion, and, at the most extreme levels, heat stroke are very real concerns when players do the amount of running that it takes to play soccer.

RICE

- Sprains are common injuries in soccer. A sprain is the stretching or partial tearing of a ligament in a joint.

- The standard treatment for a sprain or strain is RICE, an acronym for "Rest, Ice, Compression, and Elevation."

- If a player sprains his ankle (or another joint), ice it first and then wrap the injured area tightly. The wrap fulfills the "compression" part of the treatment.

- All aspects of RICE keep the swelling down and expedite the healing process.

Hydrate!

- Players can develop heat cramps, heat exhaustion, and heat stroke on hot days, and these can happen even more quickly when players are dehydrated.

- Symptoms of heat exhaustion are thirst, dizziness, and headaches.

- Heat stroke is even more dangerous, and its symptoms are disorientation, lack of sweat, and possible fever.

- If you suspect that a player is suffering from a heat-related condition, have him stop playing immediately. Get him some water and get him into the shade.

SHINGUARDS & SOCKS
The shins are the only part of the body that gets body armor

Even though equipment in soccer is minimal, guidelines for what is acceptable and what is not do exist. If a referee deems a player's equipment unacceptable, then that player is not allowed to participate in the match.

Sometimes a player may have acceptable equipment but is not wearing it properly. For instance, a player might have shinguards and socks, but the socks have fallen down, and the shinguard is exposed. If a referee notices an "equipment" problem,

he sends the player off the field to fix it after play is stopped. The referee should not stop play solely for this problem. The player may reenter the field when his equipment is fixed but not until play has been stopped again. The referee signals when it is appropriate for the player to return to the field.

The National Operating Committee on Standards for Athletic Equipment (NOCSAE) stamps the shinguards that it feels meet its standards for safety.

Velcro Shinguards

- To play in an official league, a player must wear shinguards.

- Because the bulk of the game is played with the feet, the shins are an especially vulnerable area of the body.

- A hard kick to an unprotected shin could easily result in a broken tibia. At the very least the player would get a serious contusion.

- Some shinguards are very simple and attach by a Velcro strap around the back of the calf.

Foot Strap Shinguards

- Other shinguards are part of a sleeve attached with a stirrup that goes under the foot.

- These usually have the advantage of also having ankle guards.

- Referees will require players to bend down and knock their knuckles against their shinguards to ensure their presence.

Some states are starting to require NOCSAE certification. Shinguards must be made of hard, durable plastic or rubber or some other similar material.

Slip-in Shinguards

- Some shinguards are slipped into a sleeve, which is tight enough to hold them in place.

- These tend to be smaller, a quality that many players prefer. However, these shinguards do not offer as much protection.

- These shinguards tend to be the least noticeable, and many players prefer them because they allow better ball control.

Soccer Socks

- Soccer socks are knee high. They must be long enough to cover the entire shinguards.

- Usually they are a solid color to match the uniform, although in recent years some teams wear jazzier patterns.

- Some players who don't have the type of shinguards with sleeves wear two socks, one under the shinguards and one over. Players should keep this in mind when sizing their cleats.

27

CLEATS
Find the right shoe to get the best traction on a variety of surfaces

The official rules of soccer don't require any specific footwear, but nearly every player uses some form of cleated shoe. Cleats dig into the grass, mud, or synthetic turf and help the player have better footing on the field.

Players and parents should put extra care into purchasing the perfect footwear while keeping in mind the age and ability level of the child. The youngest players do not need expensive cleats, nor do the casual weekend players. But if

a player is going to spend serious time training and playing, then she should invest in a quality shoe.

Soccer cleats are made of leather or synthetic material. Leather is more expensive but also more pliable for a better fit and more flexibility where the foot creases the shoe. Some players also contend that leather gives them a better touch on the ball. The bottoms of the cleat are made of hard molded plastic or rubber; a variety of arrangements exist.

Standard Cleats

- Standard cleats contain somewhere between twelve and twenty molded knobs on the bottom.

- These knobs are plastic or rubber. No metal cleats are allowed, and the referees will check for metal cleats before every game.

- The cleats are evenly distributed under the ball of the foot and the heel on the bottom of the shoe.

Cleats for Mud

- For muddy or wet fields, some players prefer to have the cleats primarily around the edge of the shoe.

- This configuration eliminates the clumping of wet grass or mud under the shoe, a condition that can negate the cleats' usefulness and make the shoe heavy.

- The downside is that these cleats provide too much grip if the field isn't muddy or wet. Some people also suspect that such cleats lead to more knee injuries.

- Screw-in cleats allow players to change their cleats depending on the conditions of the field.

Some players will ask if they need special shoes for synthetic turf. With today's synthetic fields, such shoes are optional, but they used to be must-haves when synthetic turf was essentially fake grass carpeting over cement. The new synthetic turf is so similar to grass that traditional cleats work fine, although there are cleats with smaller knobs.

Cleats for Turf

- Synthetic turf uses 6-inch blades of plastic grass filled with rubber pellets. The rubber allows for a cushion and provides a surface for cleats.

- Regular cleats can be worn, but shorter cleats are designed to maximize the effects of the new turf.

- Some people feel that the shorter cleats minimize knee injuries. Others feel that they really don't provide the necessary traction.

- These cleats shouldn't be used on a grass field because they don't have as much traction when used on natural surfaces.

Soccer Sleeves

- Soccer players make quite a few kicks in which the foot contacts the ball right in the area where the shoe laces are.

- A big double knot could easily mean the difference between a good kick and a bad kick, so many players use a stretchy sleeve over their laces to provide a smooth kicking surface.

- The soccer sleeves also keep the laces from coming untied.

PLAYER HEALTH

29

ENDURANCE & SPRINT TRAINING

Soccer is a running game involving long distances and short bursts of speed

In general, athletes have to be in good shape. Some sports require aerobic conditioning, whereas others require anaerobic conditioning. Many require both, and soccer leads the charge in this third category. Soccer players cover an enormous amount of ground during a match, and frequently their running is at top speed.

When an attacker is racing a defender to be the first to a ball, it's an all-out sprint. When a midfielder moves up and down the field from goal to goal, it's a long-distance run. Some studies show that soccer players run the equivalent of roughly 5 miles every game. So, it goes without saying that soccer players need to spend some part of their training time

Ladders

- Some coaches like to use ladders to increase agility.

- The ladder is a rope apparatus about 1 foot wide and 10 yards long. It is laid out on the field.

- Coaches can have the players run through the ladder, making sure the players step in each hole.

- They can vary the drill by having the players step outside the ladder and then back into the ladder. They can also have the players run backward through the ladder.

Endurance Running

- It's important to build endurance.

- Send your players out for a long group run. If you don't have a big area, four times around the field is roughly 1 mile.

- The more you can build endurance using ball handling at the same time, the better. Have players take a lap around the field while dribbling a ball.

- Younger kids seem to have limitless endurance and energy, but they have a distinct lack of patience for training, so steer away from long runs for that age group.

working on their endurance and sprinting skills.

That said, fitness training is probably everyone's least favorite part of soccer practice, so it's best if you can work on conditioning while doing drills rather than have your players do just straight running. This way the players' lung capacity and leg muscles are being trained, but the players are focusing on something else. Don't worry that it's not enough. Many drills can be very tiring as long as they're done with high intensity. Convey to your players the importance of practicing with game-level intensity. And don't forget to give them water breaks.

Rat Races

- Rat Races are a good sprinting exercise.

- The players sprint to the 6, touch it, and sprint back to the goal line. Then they sprint to the 18, touch it, and back to the goal line. Then they sprint to midfield, touch it, and sprint back to the goal line.

- You can do these exercises as individual sprints and then combine them into one long sprint.

- Relay races are a way to make sprinting more fun. You can combine the relay races with the Rat Races, too.

Game Runs

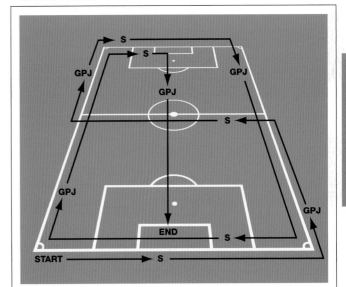

- These runs combine sprinting and endurance training, which is the most realistic simulation of what players will experience in a game.

- Players sprint where the diagram above is marked with an *S* and run in a game-paced jog where the diagram is marked with a *GPJ*.

- Players can train on their own, going to a field after hours and using this run pattern.

31

STRENGTHENING: LEGS
Strong legs make for strong kicks

Players can't kick a ball very far without strong leg muscles, so make leg-strengthening exercise part of the routine. Another reason for having strong leg muscles is that increasing evidence shows that strong muscles also protect the joints, especially the knees, from serious injury. Weightlifting is not for young kids, but that doesn't mean that you can't strengthen your players' legs during a practice.

Strong legs are a must for players, both to have endurance and to make long kicks, but these exercises shouldn't be more than ten minutes of your practice time. Not only do you need the time for more productive activities, but also you don't want to overstress players' muscles.

As players get older, encourage them to build their muscles outside of practice because these exercises should be done three times a week to be effective. Some coaches will give their players training routines to use even in the off-season.

The Lunge Walk

- The quad muscle in the front of the thigh needs to be strong. Have players try this quad-specific warm-up:

- Lunge forward with one leg, being careful not to extend the knee over the end of the foot. The knee of the back leg should touch the ground or come within 1 inch of it.

- Then take another step with the back leg, doing the same thing. This lunging walk is a great strengthener and also works on balance.

- Have your players do this walk across the width of the field.

High Knees

- A high knee run will also help strengthen the quad muscle.

- Have players run the width of the field raising their knees up to their chests.

- Not only is this a strengthening exercise, but also it helps with endurance.

- Because this is a difficult run, you'll want to mix it up with a different exercise for the run back. Have players do a side-to-side shuffle, skip, or a grapevine movement.

The grapevine is a sideways movement. The leading leg takes a step sideways, and the following leg takes a step behind. The leading leg takes another step, and then this time the following leg takes a step in front, alternating across the field.

Have some fun with this exercise by alternating leapfrogging and crawling through legs.

Leapfrog

- For young kids, turn strengthening into a game by playing Leapfrog. Have the first two players crouch down.

- The next player leapfrogs two players and crouches, creating a third obstacle, about 5 or 6 feet away. After all the players have "leapt," the first player gets up and leapfrogs them all. They progress like this across the field.

- Avoid races so the kids don't get sloppy with their leapfrogging because that's what builds the strength.

Ball Toss

- Have players incorporate a ball into a drill. In this one, players work on ball control and leg strengthening.

- Have the players throw the ball into the air, controlling it with the foot before it hits the ground.

- Then have them kneel, throw the ball up, stand up, and control it before it hits the ground. Then have them do it sitting and lying down.

- The youngest players will have trouble controlling the ball, so don't expect them to master this part of the drill. Have them just chase after the ball.

STRENGTHENING: CORE
Creating a strong soccer body is important

Most people might think that sit-ups and pushups will help a player only with throw-ins because the sport of soccer is so dominated by the legs. However, the stronger a player is, the better soccer player she will be. Coaches should train the core of a player as well.

Not only does a soccer player use the whole body when he takes shots or long passes, but also soccer is physical. Whether the player is a defender or a forward, it is important for him to win a 50/50 ball. His body will play a big part in whether he is successful or not.

Also, when a player actually has control of the ball, a defender will do his best to push him off the ball. This is a legal move as long as he is using his body to do it. If a player's core is strong, he is less likely to be pushed off the ball.

Crunches

- Sit-ups and crunches are the mainstays of core training, but make them more interesting by including a ball.

- Using the legs, the players can do crunches while gripping a ball between their feet.

- They can then try crunches while holding a ball with their knees.

- Next have players try crunches holding a ball with the hands.

- Finally, see if players can do crunches keeping the ball balanced on the stomach.

Push-ups

- Push-ups create core strength and arm strength at the same time.

- Because of the way women are built, push-ups can be very difficult for them, and many find it possible to do only bent-leg push-ups.

- The ball can be brought into this drill as well. Have the players put both hands on the ball and do a push-up on the ball.

THis exercise is very good for the body, and offers players more fun as they stretch.

PLAYER HEALTH

Two-person Sit-ups

- Strengthening exercises can be more fun if done with another person.

- Have two players lie on their backs feet to feet. One of them should have a ball.

- Now they both sit up, and the one with the ball passes it to the other one, and they lie back down.

- Another two-person drill involves having two players stand back to back about 2 feet away and twist and pass the ball to each other.

Crab Walk Soccer

- Crab Walk Soccer is a great game for the younger kids. It helps with core strengthening and is silly and fun.

- Have the kids sit down, putting their hands on the ground, behind their backs.

- Now they lift their rear ends off the ground and try to move around the field this way, using both their hands and feet.

- You can play a traditional soccer game this way (with a much smaller field, of course).

STRETCHING FOR 4- TO 6-YEAR-OLDS
Keep it loose, keep it light, and keep it fun

Flexibility is almost never a problem for four- to six-year-olds, but nonetheless, it's good to get them in the habit of warming up their muscles before they play. As their muscles develop, they'll get tighter and tighter, so flexibility drills help at any age.

Because they probably won't even feel a stretch with traditional stretching exercises, you should create stretching options under the guise of playing with the soccer ball. This

keeps it fun and goofy and starts a practice on a high note rather than on a "boring" stretching exercise.

You'll notice that all of these exercises include a ball. The more the players touch the ball, the more they'll know the ball. Their bodies and brains are sponges, and everything they learn about how the ball feels and moves will be stored for later use.

Use the ground. Unlike older kids, these players don't mind

Over/Under

- Put the children in a line, with a pile of balls in front of the first player. The players will pass the balls one at a time over their head, moving the balls from the front of the line to the back.

- Now have the kids turn around. The new front-of-

the-line player passes a ball (with his hands) between his legs to the next person.

- Reverse again and move the balls one last time, alternating over and under.

Body Parts

- This drill combines dribbling, stretching, and having fun. Each player should have his own ball.

- To start, have the players dribble around in the penalty box.

- Every minute or so, call out a new body part (e.g. foot,

head, elbow, knee, etc.). The players must stop dribbling and put this body part on the ball.

- After everyone has stopped, you should then call out "Dribble," and the players resume dribbling.

getting dirty. Slither like snakes, have them bump the ball with their noses. For this age group, anything goes.

Don't feel limited by the suggestions in this book. Try lots of different ways to have them manipulate the ball, even if it seems ridiculous. In fact, the more ridiculous, the better with this age group.

Snake

- Put the players in a line, holding the ball. The ball should touch the back of the player in front of each player.

- You are the head of the snake and now move the snake around the field. The players have to try to keep the snake from breaking.

- Next have the players put their balls onto the ground. Now the snake becomes a "follow the leader" game.

- You should mix straightforward dribbling with sharp cuts and goofy moves, such as rolling the ball with the forehead.

Roller Ball

- Have the players lie on the ground, with their ball at their heads. Have them roll the ball around their entire body ten times. This forces them to do a sit-up and to stretch forward without even noticing.

- Now have them lie back down and pass their ball around the middle of their body twenty times. They need to arch their back to get the ball under their back.

- Flip them over and do it twenty more times, getting the ball under their stomachs.

PIRATE SHIP WARM-UP

In this fun game kids work on skills without even knowing it

For the youngest children, everything needs to be a game. You want to get them warmed up without them knowing that they're warming up. Remember that you want them to be eager to come to practice and to have a love of the sport. They are too young to grasp the concept of needing to train and warm up.

For the Pirate Ship game, every player should have a ball. You'll have to do a little role playing. As the coach, you are the captain of the ship, and the players are the pirates. When you want to get their attention, you should yell, "Aye, aye, shipmates!" They should turn, face you, put one foot on the ball, and yell back "Aye, aye, captain!" They can even salute you if you'd like. In addition, you'll call out other commands, and the players will stop dribbling and perform the task at hand.

The Pirate Ship game is a perfect umbrella for both warming up the muscles and practicing many soccer skills, all while

Scrub the Deck

- You should call out this task the most of all the commands because it involves true soccer skills.

- When you yell, "Scrub the deck" the players should kick the ball between the left foot and the right foot while trying to stay in the same spot.

- This is a good opportunity to remind players of the importance of using the inside of their foot.

Raise the Sails

- When you yell "Raise the sails," the players will stop and do toe taps on the ball.

- This helps the players learn to stand on the ball of their foot and maintain balance.

- You can encourage the more advanced players to try to turn in a circle around the ball while they are toe tapping.

creating a silly, fun atmosphere. This book lists several ways to employ the "pirate" theme, but if you're creative you can expand even further. Because this game is so varied, and because the kids have such fun with this, you can do the Pirate Ship warm-up at every practice without worrying about it getting boring.

ZOOM

It's helpful if you contain your pirates in a marked area. Use the penalty box or the center circle and call it the "Pirate Ship."

Walk the Plank

- When you yell, "Walk the plank" the players should go to the edge of the "ship"—the box or the circle—and kick the ball off the ship as far as they can.

- The players then retrieve their balls.

- Because the kick is a hard one, the coach should instruct the players to make this kick using the instep. Tell the kids they should use their laces to kick the ball.

Man Overboard

- When you yell "Man overboard," it is an opportunity for players to practice their goalkeeper skills.

- The players must run to the edge of the "ship" and punt the ball.

- Now they race after the ball and dive on it. If you're lucky, some of the balls will still be moving.

39

STRETCHING FOR 7- TO 10-YEAR-OLDS
Get young soccer players into a good habit for life

As they age, soccer players need to learn the importance of stretching. It might not be too critical at this age, but every year it gets increasingly more important. So, if you're coaching seven- to ten-year-olds, stretching can get a little more focused and specific and doesn't have to be as much of a game. That doesn't mean that you can't also incorporate some of those games into your practices. These can be especially helpful in warming up the muscles before the stretch.

After the kids get warmed up, have them form a circle and begin stretching. At their age the coach should lead the stretches to make sure that the important muscles are targeted. Nonetheless, the coach should talk through the process, identifying the muscles, so the kids will eventually be able to lead the stretches on their own.

One easy way to focus on specific muscles is to work your way up the body. Start with ankles, move to calves, then

Ankle Rotation

- Ankles are a vulnerable area in soccer. The constant running, cutting, and tricky ball maneuvering frequently leave the ankle susceptible to an injury. A strong-yet-flexible ankle is no safeguard against an injury, but it does help.

- Have the kids loosen up the ankle by rotating it one way for a few rotations and then reversing directions. Have them switch feet.

- As the kids age and are capable of multitasking, you can do ankle rotation in combination with other stretches, such as mountain-climbers or arm stretches.

The Quad Muscle

- The quadriceps are the big muscles in the front of the thigh.

- To stretch it, have the kids stand on their left leg and grasp their right ankle with their right hand; they then pull their leg up as high as they can behind them. They should feel a stretch on the front of their right thigh. Have them switch legs.

- Many players struggle with balance issues with this stretch. To solve this, have players hold onto another player while they stretch.

- Another trick is to focus on a spot 5 feet out in front.

quads and hamstrings, torso, and arms. Kids will grasp the concept more quickly with a pattern to focus on.

This is often called the mountain climber stretch.

Don't have your kids stretch right off the bat. It's important to have your kids do some running, dribbling, and easy warm-up movements before they begin their stretching. Stretching a warm muscle is much safer and more effective than stretching a cold muscle.

Calf Muscles

- Have the kids lie on the ground, as if going to do a push-up. Then they press up so that the arms and legs are both straight, creating a V shape or mountain shape with the body.

- Now have the kids press the right heel down to the ground. Have them feel the stretch in the calf. They hold the stretch for ten seconds and then switch to the left leg.

- To stretch the lower part of their calf, have the kids bend the knee slightly. Have them do this as a separate stretch or before switching legs.

Hamstring

- The muscle on the back of the thigh is called the "hamstring." This is the muscle that you stretch when you touch your toes.

- One way to isolate the hamstring on a single leg is to cross the legs at the ankles. When your players bend to touch their toes, they are stretching only the hamstring on the back leg. Have them switch legs.

- Also have them stretch the hamstring by sitting on the ground and reaching out toward the toes. Have them bend one knee in to isolate a single leg.

WARM-UP DRILLS

BULLS IN THE RING

This warm-up workout addresses dribbling, ball control, passing, and fun

A great way to warm up the kids is to have them work on their dribbling skills. These can use constant attention. Straight dribbling, however, can be a little boring, so you need to spice it up a little. Bulls in the Ring gives you lots of flexibility to work on many aspects of dribbling and at the same time to create a variety of games to keep it interesting.

Begin by having all the players in the center circle. This is the ring, and they are the bulls. Every player should have her own ball for this drill. If you have access to only half a field for practice, you can use the penalty box instead, calling it "Bulls in the Box."

Although this drill seems like a straight dribbling drill, a pro-

Easy Dribbling

- Have everyone dribble in the enclosed area. After the kids are comfortable, add a few challenges.

- Have the kids dribble only with the outside of their feet or alternate, inside and outside. Have them dribble only with their left feet or roll the ball with the under-side of their feet.

- You can also have them change speeds.

- For competition, tell them to sprint out of the ring with their ball. They must put their foot on the ball when they leave the ring; the last one to do that loses.

Fakes in the Ring

- Taking the dribbling up another level, you should have all the players do fakes. The dribbling chapter has a number of fakes you can teach them.

- Call out different fakes every thirty seconds or so.

- You can also tell the kids to stop and toe tap.

- You can have them throw the ball up into the air, get it under control, and then keep dribbling.

gression takes it from a simple dribbling exercise to a more complicated exercise, and then eventually it turns it into a fun game at the end. Also, it's important to bring the fun into it by playing up the "bull" theme. Kids get bored easily by repetition and drilling, so if they view it as a silly game instead, you'll hold their attention much longer. Feel free to change the animal if you find you're able to be more creative that way.

Passing

- Now that you've worked on individual ball control skills, you can add a little passing to the mix.

- On your call, have the kids change balls with someone else. Make it a competition so that they're eager to stay spread out. Kids in a clump will have a hard time exchanging balls.

- Have the kids pass to another player and then get both themselves and their new ball out of the box.

Competition

- Add some defense to the mix. Have players kick the other players' balls out of the ring while maintaining possession of their own ball.

- If a ball goes out of the ring, the bull also goes out. The last one left is the winner.

- Some players passively dribble and let the others do the dirty work.

- In that case, designate a couple of "matadors" to attack the bulls. These matadors don't have a ball. Their only job is to get rid of the bulls.

STRETCHES FOR 11- TO 14-YEAR-OLDS

Stretching is serious business and should be done before every practice and game

The body-changing years are the time when coaches really need to focus on the stretching habit. This is when muscles are developing at a faster rate, the ligaments, tendons, and muscles are all tightening up, and the intensity levels are rising. Put it all together, and it's a recipe for more injuries.

Because kids change at different rates and different ages,

quite a few of your players won't need as much stretching and warm-up as others, but this fact shouldn't deter you from creating an environment in which stretching and warm-ups are a regular routine. You should be sure that they are an integral part of every practice and pregame warm-up.

All the stretching and warm-ups that have been described

Arm Stretches

- Although the arms aren't the most important part of the soccer body, players still have to use them for throw-ins, so it's a good idea to stretch them.

- Have the players grab their elbow with the opposite hand and pull the arm across the body. Have them hold it

for ten seconds. Then have them switch sides.

- Now have the players grab their elbow and push it behind their head.

- Finally, have the players clasp the hands behind the back and pull up with both arms.

Inner Thigh

- To let the kids stretch the groin muscles, have them sit on the ground with their feet touching each other. Have them bring their feet in close to the body and try to press the knees to the ground.

- Lunges also stretch the inner thigh and groin. Have the kids stand with legs spread.

Have them bend the knee to one side. Let them feel the stretch in the inner thigh of the straight leg.

- Now have them face the bent knee and press the front of the back leg into the ground. This stretches the muscle on the front of the thigh.

for the four-to-six age group and the seven-to-ten age group can be used for this group as well. This spread will just give you more stretches to add to the program. Stretching is cumulative.

Another hips stretch: Have the kids lie on their back. Have them bend both knees, putting the right ankle on top of the left knee. Have them pull the left leg into the chest until they feel the stretch in their right hip. Have them switch legs.

Hamstring Stretch

- The hamstring is a hard muscle to stretch really well. Many players have very tight hamstrings. One way to get an extra stretch is to have two players work on each other.

- Have one player lie on the ground. He should bend one leg, which helps him keep his lower back on the ground. Then he should raise the other leg straight up into the air.

- The teammate now pushes on that leg, providing more stretch than the player could do by himself.

The Pretzel Stretch

- The pretzel stretch works the outside of the hips. Have the kids sit on the ground with the legs extended. Have them cross the right leg over the left, placing the right foot up by the left thigh. Have them bend the left knee back so that the left foot is near the right hip. Have them turn toward that left hip and try to place the left elbow behind the right knee. Hence the term *pretzel stretch*!

- Have the kids hold the stretch and then reverse the pretzel.

HALF-AND-HALF DRILL

Use warm-ups to work on ever-important ball control

The Half-and-Half drill gets its name from the fact that half the team has the ball, and half the team doesn't at all times. But throughout this drill, the ball is constantly changing possession. Communication is key in this drill, so that only one ball goes to one player. Both passer and receiver should be talking.

This drill should be played in a small contained area to increase the touches on the ball. Whether he has a ball or not,

a player should always be moving and looking for an open space. This is another good reason to confine the area because it really makes the kids work for it.

In all four parts of this drill there are passers and receivers. The passers and receivers both have additional responsibilities. After a passer has sent the ball off, he must move to an open space. After a receiver has controlled the ball, he must accelerate forward.

Dribbling and Passing

- Players with the ball will take two touches and pass it to a player who is open.

- The player who just received the ball makes a turn, accelerates, and then looks for an open player again.

- This process should continue until the players' heart rates are elevated.

Thigh Control

- Players starting with the ball will toss it underhand to an open player's thigh.

- The player controls the ball, brings it down to his foot, and then accelerates.

- After acceleration, the player then picks up the ball and tosses it to an open player.

The acceleration aspect of the drill is just as important as the ball control aspect. The players need to get used to moving quickly the instant they receive a ball. It is also important for the players to run through the ball while getting it under control. Coaches should not neglect this fact. Players need to practice under conditions that are as gamelike as possible.

Chests

- Players starting with the ball will toss it underhand to an open player's chest. A player should "catch" the ball on the hard area, just below the neck.

- The player controls the ball, brings it down to his foot, and then accelerates.

- After acceleration, the player then picks up the ball and tosses it to an open player.

Heads

- Players with the ball will keep the ball during this part of the drill. They'll exchange after five tosses.

- Players without the ball will run toward the player with the ball and head the ball back to the tosser.

- Players should change teammates with every toss.

- Tossers should vary the height of the ball.

WARM-UP DRILLS

MECHANICS

Use the inside, outside, and sole of the foot to move the ball

Dribbling is probably the first skill that all coaches teach to their players. In fact, dribbling is such a natural movement that you almost don't have to teach it at all. It's simple, and it forms the base for the rest of the game. A player may use every part of the body except the area from the shoulders down to the fingertips.

Many young players find dribbling with the inside of their foot much simpler than using the outside of the foot or the bottom of the foot, so they just don't use these parts of their feet. This is a bad habit to get into because so many fakes and turns depend on the use of other parts of the foot. With every dribbling drill you do with your players, be sure they are using all parts of both feet.

You also need to focus on intensity. Dribbling at slow speeds is fairly simple. Dribbling without anyone challenging is also simple. It gets much trickier when a player is trying

Beginning to Dribble

- Have players move the ball around a designated area. Most of them will use the inside of their feet. Be sure to stop the ones who try to kick the ball with their toes.

- After they dribble for a while, show the players that they can also use the shoelace area to push the ball forward. Have them try that with both feet.

- Now show them the outside of the foot and the underside. Make the players understand that they should use every part of the foot.

Outside and Under

- Have players get comfortable with the outside and bottom of the foot.

- Set up dribbling drills in which the players may use only the outside of their feet. Have them dribble around in the penalty box or through a slalom course of cones.

- Have them drag the ball down the field using the bottom of their feet. Have them go one way, then reverse feet and come back.

- A combination of the two moves works well. Have the kids dribble forward once with the outside of the foot, then drag the ball sideways.

to dribble under gamelike conditions. Another way to create game-level intensity is to add a defender to the mix.

Have them do this all at once or set up a relay race situation.

High-speed Dribbling

- Part of dribbling practice should include game-condition dribbling at high speed or under duress.

- Stress the importance of balancing speed with control. Players need to be able to go fast but keep the ball near their feet.

- Have your kids run Rat Races with the ball. Because they have to turn and go back at each line, those players who dribble too far out in front will be penalized.

With a Defender

- Teach your players how to shield the ball with their body; if they always keep their body between the defender and the ball, the defender has a hard time getting at the ball.

- Pair up your players, one ball for each pair.

- One player dribbles across the field, shielding the entire time. The defender should make it difficult but should not try to steal the ball.

- Now take it up another notch. Allow the defender to steal the ball. The players can use shielding, fakes, or any other dribbling moves.

MOVES

Use lunges, turns, fakes, and every other trick to fool the defender

Moves are complicated footwork that will help your players escape a defender. However, because they are complicated, they will take lots of teaching and practice for your players to master them.

When you teach a move, you first want to model the move. If you are not a soccer star yourself, find a player who knows how to do the move so that the kids are able to see what the move looks like when it's successfully executed.

The next step is to have the demonstrator break the move down into small steps. While he's doing this, each player should have a ball and try to copy each movement. After players are comfortable with each step, you should have them try to put it all together. During this time, you can work with individual players who are struggling.

Every move should be practiced with both the left foot and the right foot. And all players should be encouraged to do

Drag-back

- One of the most basic dribbling moves is called a "drag-back." This move allows the player to reverse direction.

- While dribbling, the player steps on the ball with the top of her foot. This stops the ball from rolling.

- Now the player drags the ball back in the opposite direction, turning her body as soon as she does this.

- If the player uses her right foot to drag back, she should turn to the right. If she uses her left foot, she should turn to the left.

The L Turn

- The L turn can be used with the inside of the foot or the outside of the foot. It's another turn that allows the player to reverse direction.

- The dribbler should plant one foot next to the ball. He then places his other foot in front of the ball, making an L with his two feet.

- The foot in front of the ball pushes the ball backward in the opposite direction.

- The player then turns his body as well.

each move at full speed after they are comfortable with the move itself. Practicing at home will help players improve.

The dribbler should lunge with his body to make this fake convincing.

The Scissors Move

- The player plants the left foot next to the ball.

- He swings his right foot over the ball and hits the ball with the outside of his right foot, pushing it to the right. (This can be done reversing the left and right feet as well.)

- The defender assumes that the right foot is going to hit the ball with the inside of the foot, pushing the ball to the right; he is taken by surprise.

The Maradona

- This move is called the "Maradona" after a famous Argentinean player. It's one of the trickier moves that can be tried after the players have mastered the more basic moves.

- The move begins by stopping the dribble with the bottom of the right foot.

- The player then moves the right foot over to the other side of the ball.

- Now the player spins counterclockwise over the top of the ball and pulls the ball with the bottom of her left foot by scraping it across the top of the ball.

DRIBBLING

DRILLS FOR 4- TO 6-YEAR-OLDS

Keep it fun, keep it silly, and teach kids skills at the same time

Four- to six-year-old players are not necessarily on the soccer field because soccer is their idea of a great time. Maybe if they have older siblings, they've been kicking a ball around in the backyard and are looking forward to getting a chance to play themselves, but the majority of preschoolers are playing the game because their parents thought it would be a good idea.

If you're coaching children of this age, you may be dealing with players who have never seen a soccer ball before. You may be dealing with kids who still have separation anxiety and are petrified to be taking orders from a stranger. You will certainly be dealing with soccer players who have a very short attention span. All of this should come into play when you think about how you want to structure your practices. Even if it were a parent who put the four-year-old on the field with you, you need to turn it around such that the kid himself

Driving School

- Everyone should have a ball).

- Call out a variety of phrases:

1. Left turn: Players turn left.

2. Right turn: Players turn right.

3. U-turn: Players reverse direction.

4. Traffic jam: Players stand in place and toe tap on ball.

5. Raceway: Players dribble while sprinting.

6. Head-on collision: Players stop and put their heads on the ball.

Nutmeg Races

- For this drill, divide the team into two groups. All the players in one of the groups should have a ball.

- The other group stands still with legs open all around a grid or the goal box.

- Players with a ball get one minute to dribble the ball

and pass it through the open legs. This is called a "nutmeg." They then retrieve their ball and try again.

- The player with the most nutmegs in one minute wins. Then have the players switch groups.

thinks it's a great idea to be there.

To begin with, get the kids moving right off the bat. Don't start by talking because you're going to bore them, lose their focus, and give nervous children the opportunity to start looking for Mommy. It helps if you can be silly right off the bat, too. After you get children giggling while they are playing, you won't have to worry.

Red Light, Green Light

- Every player should have a ball and be lined up on the end line.

- You stand at midfield and turn your back on the players, yelling "Green light," which indicates the players may dribble forward.

- You then yell "Red light" and turn around. All players must stop their ball, put a foot on it, and freeze. Any players who are caught chasing after their ball have to go back to the beginning.

- This drill teaches players to keep their dribbles close to their body.

Slalom

- Having young kids dribble through a course helps them learn ball control.

- Divide the kids into two or three groups. Set up the slalom course—cones in a line about 6 feet apart from each other in front of each group—and have the kids dribble through.

- After a while, have them do a race through the course. They must navigate the course and bring the ball back to the next team-mate, who then has to do the same thing until every player on the team has gone.

DRILLS FOR 7- TO 10-YEAR-OLDS
Step up the skill level but still keep it fun

Coaching the seven- to ten-year-old age group gets tricky. The attention span of some of these children is still at the level of preschoolers. Others can start focusing on one particular skill for a long period of time.

Skills also vary. By this age players are choosing to play soccer rather than having it thrust upon them by eager parents. Of course, there will always be those who are there reluctantly, but by this age many know what the game is all about

and are eager to play. Some are even playing pickup games at recess or after school. Because of this, player skills start to vary dramatically at this age. It will be obvious to you who plays soccer at recess and in the backyard and who gets their only exposure to the ball and the game at your practice.

Some leagues divide their teams up by skill at this age. Others have their teams mixed. Lucky for you if you have a team with compatible players, but don't despair if your team

Red Rover

- Line the team members up on the goal line, with the target being the midfield line, with a player in the middle.

- The middle player calls out "Red Rover, Red Rover, let the blue shirts come over!" Anyone with a blue shirt must try to dribble through

the middle and get to the other line safely.

- If a player loses his balls he goes in the middle, too.

- Players can use any category to call out the dribblers—shirt color, hair color, first names, and so forth.

Relay Races

- Divide the players into two or three even teams.

- You can set up a variety of dribbling challenges, depending on which skill you want to work on.

- Have the kids roll the ball with the underside of the

shoe or have them dribble through cones. You can have them do straight sprinting to a line, or you can have them do Rat Races, which require them to keep tighter control of the ball because they have to change direction.

is more of the latter kind. These drills work for either group. Games are fun for everyone, and the added challenge of a competition rather than a drill might inspire some of your players to work a little harder outside of practice.

Criss-Cross

- Divide the team into two groups. Every player should have a ball.

- The teams line up at opposite ends of the box. (They should be on the short sides of the goal box.)

- At your whistle, all the players dribble across the penalty box to the other side, trying to avoid the other team coming at them with their balls.

- The team that reaches the other side first, lined up on the line, with their feet on their balls, is the winner.

Circle Dribbling

- Have the players begin the drill by dribbling around the outside of the circle all in the same direction.

- As the players dribble, shout out the following commands:

Jog: Players should dribble at a comfortable speed.

Full speed: Players should dribble at top speed.

Cut: Players should cut the ball in the other direction and travel around the circle.

Cross: All players should cut across the circle, avoiding contact with other players or other players' balls.

DRILLS FOR 11- TO 14-YEAR-OLDS
Step up the drills and the skills to create fabulous ball handlers

When you're coaching eleven- to fourteen-year-olds, the hardest thing to deal with is the prepubescent and teenager mind-set. In their minds, they know it all. Some may even think they know more than you. And if you have a child on the team, then there's a chance that there's at least someone who thinks you know nothing.

The biggest challenge is that players have been doing dribbling drills since they were four. They don't think they need to

practice dribbling anymore. It's boring. They want to scrimmage and play their favorite games. But don't give in. There are always new moves, and kids can always improve on their foot skills, no matter what their playing level.

That said, you do need to allow for some flexibility at this age. Give the kids a chance to be on their own, making plans, talking about the day, and generally being unsupervised. A warm-up run and stretching time are perfect times for this to

King of the Hill

- Every player has a ball and dribbles around in the penalty box.

- Each player focuses on protecting his own ball while trying to eliminate the balls of his opponents.

- After a ball leaves the box, the player it belonged to is

eliminated. The last player left with a ball is the winner.

- If you do this with teams, it's a faster game. A player who loses his ball can stay in the box and help his team eliminate the other balls.

Through the Legs

- Divide your players into groups of four. In each group, two players are designated the dribblers, while the other two players stand with their legs apart and are designated the goals—one goal for each dribbler. They should stand about 20 yards apart from each other.

- The players in the middle battle with some one-on-one dribbling, trying to get the ball into the opponents' goal.

- After two minutes, have the goals and the dribblers switch places.

happen. Tell the kids that you're giving them time to chat and that then they need to focus. You can also make it clear that if they don't pay attention and focus after stretching, then they lose that privilege.

One versus One

- Basic one-on-one dribbling is the best way to work on faking, turning, and keeping the ball close.

- Divide players into pairs. One player should be on the end line with the ball. The other should be opposite her, about 30 yards out. Mark this line with cones or pinnies.

- As the end line player starts dribbling, the other rushes in to try to steal the ball. Each player tries to get the ball across the other player's line. Have the players take turns starting with the ball.

Breakaway

- Breakaway not only works on dribbling skills but also helps to teach the kids to become more aggressive.

- Have two players lie down on the field with their feet toward the goal. Roll the ball out between them and yell "Go."

- The players have to scramble to their feet and race to the ball, fighting to be the one to dribble and shoot on the goal.

DRIBBLING

GAMES FOR ALL
Add some competition but still keep it fun

No matter what their age, children should enjoy the sport of soccer. Isn't that why they are playing in the first place? Both their practices and their games should be focused on both fun and learning. They are not mutually exclusive.

One development over the last few decades is the pressure that is placed on children to hone their skills to a degree that they can perform at the highest levels. Sports are looked at as vehicles to success—status in high school, acceptance into top colleges, and for a select few even possible career paths. Although this thinking has some validity, it's not healthy. We put too much pressure on our kids to become superstars, even at a very young age. Sports are created to provide healthy outlets and alternatives to the daily stresses we all face, and that includes children, too.

If parents and coaches will look back at their own less-structured childhood, they'll realize that what made the sport fun

Turkey Tag

- This drill is especially loved by younger players.

- For this drill every player will need a ball and a pinny. The pinny is tucked into the shorts.

- Players dribble around and try to grab the pinny out of the shorts of another player, thereby eliminating that player. The last one left is the winner.

- You can also turn this into a team tag game if you have two sets of different-colored pinnies.

Bulldog

- Every player has a ball and lines up on the end line. You are the first bulldog.

- The players now try to dribble across to the other side of the penalty box.

- The bulldog tries to steal the balls, barking and growling at the players. This part is especially important for the little players. It makes all the difference in the enjoyment of the game.

- If a player loses his ball, he becomes a bulldog as well. Play continues until everyone becomes a bulldog.

were the competition and the sport itself. Endless drilling was not part of the pickup game in the park. Practices can be instructional and fun if you make an effort.

So as a coach, no matter what the level of your players, you have to keep it fun. Playing games is the best way to do this.

If the marauders have a hard time getting started, you can help them at first.

Marauder

- Start with only three players who don't have a ball. These players are the marauders. They are the defenders.

- Each marauder tries to steal a ball. After she succeeds, she attempts to score on the goal, which is in the middle of the playing area. If the marauder scores the goal, the player whose ball was stolen becomes a marauder, too.

- Play continues until the last player with the ball wins.

Kings (or Queens)

- Divide the players into two teams. One player from each team is a king (put a pinny on his head) and stands in the half-circle above the penalty box.

- The players try to hit each other with the balls. If a player is hit, he is "captured" and has to stand with his legs spread out.

- The king frees the player by crawling through his legs. Then that player becomes the king.

- A team wins by hitting the king with the ball when he leaves the castle.

DRIBBLING

MECHANICS
Teach your players how to get a moving ball under control

It's one thing to control the ball when you have it in your possession. It's quite another when the ball is traveling toward you at high speed. Teaching your players ball control is critical to having a good team. Your players need to be able to use their feet, thighs, chest, and head to bring the ball to a point where it's under their control.

Begin with the foot. In most of the world, the sport of soccer is called "football" because so much of the action is done with the foot. Not only do the players move the ball with their foot, but also it's the easiest way for them to get control of the ball when it's moving. After they've mastered that, they can move on to other parts of the body because the principle is the same.

No matter what part of the body players use, they have to view it as a cushion for the ball. If they're "catching" the ball with their thigh, the players have to keep their legs firm but

Using the Foot

- If the ball is on the ground, have your players turn the inside of the foot toward the ball and raise their foot up about 4 inches off the ground, which should be about halfway up the ball.

- If their foot is too low, the ball will roll over the foot,

and if it's too high, the ball might force itself under the foot. Practice will help players find the right level.

- The players should "give" a little with their foot as soon as the ball hits it.

Ball from the Air

- Here players can use the top or the inside part of their foot.

- Be sure your players get their foot under the ball this time while lifting their foot 4 inches off the ground.

- With space between their foot and the ground, play-

ers can "give" with the ball, making for a cushioned landing.

- Some find it easier to take a ball with their thigh, a bigger and softer surface that provides more opportunity to settle the ball. Players should have their thigh drop down at impact.

with a little give. They don't want to have their legs be a wall that the ball can bounce off. The instant the ball makes contact, the player should relax the leg a little and allow the ball to push back some. This will slow the ball without causing it to ricochet.

Using the Chest

- A player may also "catch" the ball with his chest. He should arch his back and catch the ball just below the chest.

- Frequently the ball will be bouncing, and a player can use his chest to knock the ball down.

- In this case, he should lean forward and use his body's momentum to propel the ball down onto the ground and in the direction he wants to go.

The Head

- Although players are more likely to use their head to pass or redirect the ball, it is possible for them to use their head to control the ball and bring it down to their feet.

- The player needs to keep her head and neck firm and allow her body to be the part that caves a little and creates the cushion. A loose neck is a recipe for whiplash.

- Players under the age of twelve should not use their head at all.

61

STRATEGY
Teach players to use the brain before they even touch the ball

Mastering ball control is one thing. It's another thing altogether to be able to do it well in a game situation. It would be nice if the opponents allowed your players to take their time to get the ball under control, but this will almost never be the case, so your players have to learn to adapt their ball control skills to a game that's played at high speed and under pressure.

Because your players will be challenged for every ball, insist

that they take the ball out of the air. If instead they plan to wait for the ball to bounce, some better-trained player on the other team is going to step in and get it first. Unfortunately, in the beginning many players are reluctant to do this—especially if it's a high or fast-moving ball—thinking that it might hurt. You must insist on this in order to break that natural tendency.

Players will also have a natural tendency to use one foot

Split-second Decisions

- Control it with the foot?

- Control it with the thigh?

- Run through it with the chest?

- Head the ball away?

- Use one touch or two?

No Bounces

- If players let the ball bounce, a player from the other team will get to the ball first while your players wait for it to hit the ground.

- Or, assuming that the ball is coming with enough force, the ball will hit the ground and bounce over your players.

- Have consequences every time a player avoids taking the ball out of the air.

- A player might have to do push-ups or sit-ups or run a lap, for example.

more than the other. Unfortunately, the soccer ball won't always cooperate with that tendency. The ball is going to come from both the right and the left, and the ball will need to be distributed with both the right foot and left foot. Players who aren't using both sides of their bodies to control the ball will be at a serious disadvantage.

Learning one-touch control takes some practice, so practice often.

Game Speed Control

- If a player is running forward, and the ball drops directly in front of her feet, she will trip or run right past it.

- Therefore, players should practice controlling the ball on the move with all parts of the body. Using the torso to control the ball is especially effective in this situation.

- To get control with her body, the player should "run through" the ball, hitting it firmly with her chest.

- If she leans forward, the ball will be forced down onto the ground in front of her.

One-touch Control

- Most of the ball control so far has been directed at dropping the ball in front of the body, where a player can then make a decision to dribble, pass, or shoot.

- This is called "two-touch ball control": one touch to get the ball under control and one touch to move.

- One-touch ball control, however, involves the player's redirecting the ball—either as a pass or a shot—the first time he touches the ball.

- He doesn't dribble before the ball touches his body.

63

DRILLS FOR 4- TO 6-YEAR-OLDS
Combine instruction with fun to get the ball under control

Ball control for the preschool group is not too tricky. The ball doesn't move at a fast pace for these young players, so there's not much they need to do to slow it down and get it under control. The preschoolers are so little, and by comparison the ball is so big that the main challenge is getting the ball moving, not getting the ball under control. Nonetheless, it's something you can teach through games and drills because it always helps to start at a young age.

Before you can begin the games, however, you do have to do a little instruction on the mechanics. Whenever you instruct with this age group, though, you have to keep it short and sweet. No long demonstrations and lectures.

The best way to do this is to give a quick one- or two-sentence instruction with a little demonstration. Then have the kids practice on their own. Now is the time to walk around and give individual instruction to each child rather than lec-

Toss It Up

- To get kids comfortable controlling the ball out of the air, have them throw it up into the air themselves.

- Every child should have a ball. Spend five minutes having them practice catching the ball with their feet before it hits the ground.

- Kids can practice ball control on their own, which means if they want to improve they're not limited to just practices and clinics.

- They have to spend ten minutes throwing the ball up into the air and catching it when they're at home.

Playing Catch

- Now divide the players into pairs, one ball for each pair.

- Have them pass the ball back and forth, focusing on stopping the ball directly in front of them.

- After they've mastered the ball rolling along the ground, you can have them toss the ball to each other. See if they can catch the ball with their thighs or chest.

ture to them as a group. They'll be able to focus more, and you'll be able to tailor your advice to their specific needs.

Kickball

- Divide the players into two teams. Use disks or pinnies to mark off the bases.

- The "pitcher" should kick, or pass, the ball to the "batter," who kicks the ball and runs around the bases.

- The other players have to field the ball with their feet and either hit the player with the ball or get it to the base before the player.

- If the players cannot get anyone out, run through the line-up just once, then switch sides.

Superheroes

- Every player has a ball. Have each player pick a superhero.

- A player will throw you the ball, which you will then throw into the air. The object is for the player to control the ball before it hits the ground in order to save the world.

- If the ball hits the ground, the player turns into a villain who tries to take other superheroes' balls out of the air. After one attempt, a player goes back to being a superhero.

DRILLS FOR 7- TO 10-YEAR-OLDS
More touches on the ball lead to improved ball control abilities

Players age seven to ten have a huge range of developmental abilities, but for almost all of them their progress in soccer grows by leaps and bounds. The more touches that they can have on the ball, the more they'll start to figure out how the ball moves and what they can do to manipulate it.

This is why it's important to teach them the art of juggling around this age. If they can manipulate the ball and get a sense of the touch that's needed to keep the ball aloft, they'll be much more attuned to the type of touch needed on the field.

Except for juggling, you aren't going to teach ball control in isolation. In a game situation, players will necessarily always have to do something with the ball after they get it under control. Fortunately, most ball control drills will work on two areas at once. Players will control the ball and then pass it. Or they'll control it and then dribble. Or control it and shoot.

Juggling

- Juggling the ball in soccer entails keeping the ball aloft using the feet, thighs, chest, and head.

- Players try to get as many touches as they can before the ball hits the ground.

- Although juggling may not seem to translate to game play, it's actually an incredibly useful tool to train children in ball handling.

- Juggling is something that the players can also do at home.

Three-player Drill

- Divide players into groups of three approximately 10 feet apart. The two end players have a ball, but the middle player doesn't.

- One end player passes the ball in to the middle player, who controls it and passes it back. The middle player then spins around to receive the ball from the other player.

- The third player needs to be passing the ball right before the middle player turns.

- Vary the drill by making it one-touch passing or by having the outside players toss the ball into the air.

And so on. Actually, every aspect of practice will be "teaching" them ball control skills. The game is the best teacher of all.

Soccer Tennis

- Believe it or not, this drill isn't done on a tennis court but rather across a line on the field, having players imagine the net.

- Have two players on each side of the "net." Team 1 serves the ball. Team 2 controls the ball and then kicks the ball back.

- They continue this volleying until either the ball does not go into the air or the ball bounces twice.

- You can even keep score the way you do in tennis.

Punt and Catch

- This drill combines the keeper's punting practice with the players' ball control.

- The keeper punts the ball; the first player in line controls that ball out of the air.

- If he succeeds, then he dribbles it back to the keeper and goes to the end of the line.

- If he lets the ball bounce first, however, then he has to dribble around the field instead. This is a great motivator for getting underneath that punt.

DRILLS FOR 11- TO 14-YEAR-OLDS
Take ball control skills to the next level

By the time players are eleven to fourteen years of age, they should have mastered the basic ball control skills. Now they're ready to take it to the next level. They need to be able to control the ball effectively under pressure from a defender and at high speed.

Any drill you do with this age should always be done under matchlike conditions. You need to either include a defender, reduce the touches, or have your players performing the drill while moving at top speed. The added benefit of this is that your players will be getting in shape at the same time that they're working on ball control skills.

It's always important to keep the practices fun and enjoyable, but you don't have to worry about making every single drill fit the "fun" category. Most players are on the field because they love soccer and want to be there. These days you won't get too many completely new players in the eleven-to-

One-touch Passing

- Players should pair up, one ball for each pair. Have the players stand 10 feet apart. Spend two minutes allowing two-touch passing just to get them warmed up.

- Next have your players pass back and forth without stopping the ball.

- Stress the importance of accuracy over speed and strength. You can even make it a competition—see which pair can do it the longest.

- Now move the players apart a bit. See if they can continue accurate one-touch passing when they're kicking the ball harder.

The Shifting Game

- Divide players into two even lines facing each other about 6 feet apart.

- One line has balls and spreads out with about 6 feet between them. This line remains stationary.

- The other line receives the ball and passes it back to the same player with one touch, then shifts down to the next player to do it again.

- The player at the end sprints back to the beginning. When the line gets back to where it started, switch sides.

fourteen age range. These are experienced players who want to improve, and most are willing to work a little at it.

Do this again and again, switching from feet to thighs to chests to heads.

Group Juggling

- If your players are experienced jugglers, they should be fairly adept at keeping the ball aloft.

- Divide your players into groups. Someone begins juggling in each group. After one or two touches, he sends the ball to someone else.

- The groups can compete to see who can keep the ball aloft the longest.

- Tell the players that they can have unlimited touches at a time or direct them to have only one, two, or three touches before they have to pass off the ball.

Throw-in Drill

- Divide the players into two groups: a line of throwers and a line of receivers.

- Players should practice throwing the ball to the receiver's foot. They don't want to hit the player in the stomach with a hard throw.

- The receiver controls the ball and dribbles over to the thrower line.

- A variation of this drill could include practicing the long throw that a player runs onto down the sideline.

GAMES FOR ALL
Use familiar games to teach skills

You may notice that many of the games and drills in this book sound familiar. A lot of them are based on games that children might play on the playground. They might also be based on other sports. There are two reasons for this.

First, giving players lots of instructions is not only long but also boring. If you have to spend fifteen minutes of precious practice time explaining the rules of a new game, that's fifteen minutes that the kids aren't learning soccer skills.

Long instructions also tend to fall on deaf ears. One coaching theory is that girls will listen to roughly two sentences, and boys will listen to about two words. Either way, long instructions aren't going to be effective.

So you need to take advantage of the knowledge the kids already have in their little brains. If you say, "We're playing tag," you don't have to explain much—only the variation you're adding to it.

Spud

- Give everyone a number. Throw the ball up into the air and call out a number. The player with that number retrieves and controls the ball and yells "Stop." The others sprint away until they hear "Stop," at which point they freeze.

- Now she has to pass the ball and hit another player. That hit person gets an *S* (the start of *S-P-U-D*). If the kicker misses, she gets an *S*.

- The kicker now starts the game over by throwing the ball up and calling another number.

Steal the Bacon

- Divide players into two teams, each with its own goal marked by cones placed about 10 yards apart. Place goals 18 yards apart.

- Give each player a number that matches the number of a player on the other team. Now call out a number and throw out a ball.

- Each team's player with that number races to get the ball across the other team's goal line.

- Players on the goal line control the ball without using their hands and pass it back to their teammate on the field.

Second, these games are already proven successes. Why reinvent the wheel? If a game has been popular for decades, then it's probably a pretty good game. It might have to be adapted slightly for soccer play, but it's fundamentally the same fun game that it is on the playground.

ZOOM

A variation you can use is to reward the player who controls the ball out of the air. If he does, he gets three dribbles. If he doesn't, he stays where he is.

Circle Ball

- This drill is done in the center circle. Divide players into two groups. One group is on the perimeter of the circle. The other group is in the middle. Every player on the circle has a ball.

- Players throw the ball to a player inside the circle.

The player inside the circle controls the ball and passes it to someone else on the other side of the circle.

- Players throwing the ball in should vary the placement and height of the ball.

Wall Ball

- If you have access to a wall or backboard, you can play Wall Ball. Players get in a line about 20 feet out from the wall.

- The first player has two touches to get the ball under control and back to

the wall for the next player in line. One touch should be to stop the ball and one to kick it.

- If he fails, then he's eliminated. The last player left in line is the winner.

71

SHORT BALL
Short, accurate passing keeps the ball away from opponents

Soccer is a team game, so you want to encourage your players to work as a team. That means lots of passing. Tell your players that soccer is really a giant game of Keep Away. Point out to your players that if the other team never has the ball, it can't score.

Of course, in a regular game of Keep Away, the teams won't be balanced. It's usually a big group trying to keep something away from one or two. Or, in Monkey in the Middle, two people keep the ball away from one. There's always an imbalance. In soccer, of course, the numbers are balanced, which makes the game a little trickier, but the players will just have to be that much more skilled and creative.

In soccer the ball can go forward, backward, and sideways as long as it's kept away from the other team. Again, if your players picture the game as Keep Away, then they won't be so reluctant to look behind them for a pass. This is a very hard

Inside of the Foot

- When a player wants to make a short, accurate pass, he should use the inside of his foot.

- This part of the foot doesn't provide a tremendous amount of power, but because so much of the foot contacts the ball, it improves the accuracy of the pass.

- This should be a pass that stays on the ground.

- Have players pass back and forth this way for a bit. Then have them pass as they move down the field so they get the concept of leading the player.

Contact on the Ball

- When making an inside-of-the-foot pass, a player should contact the ball in the middle.

- If anything, he should err on the side of slightly higher than the middle. If he contacts the ball on the lower side, the ball will pop up into the air.

- Learning the right amount of power to put behind the pass is something that comes with experience and practice.

concept for young players to grasp. They feel that the ball should always be going forward toward the goal.

Accuracy is important when you're playing Keep Away. An ambiguous pass is an invitation to the defense to step in and steal the ball. However, an accurate pass doesn't always mean a pass that goes from one player to the foot of his teammate. If the teammate is running, the passer will want to send the ball a little in front of the runner so the runner won't have to stop and break stride. This tactic is called "leading" a player and is something that your team will learn only by doing passing drills on the move. You can really give them a sense of "leading" by pairing them up, one ball to a pair, and having them run the length of the field, passing to each other. They will soon grasp that it's easier if the ball is sent at in front.

Outside of the Foot

- The outside of the foot is good for a short pass as well. In fact, generally it's good for a pass that will be even shorter.

- This pass is more of a quick snap and used to nudge the ball around a defender when a teammate is nearby.

- Again, contact should be in the middle of the ball.

Heel Pass

- The heel pass is almost like a handoff. It's a short pass to a teammate to escape a defender.

- The player steps over the ball and uses the backswing to provide momentum, snapping his heel into the ball.

- To practice, have one player dribble down the field with a teammate trailing. Another player is the defender.

- When the defender attacks, the player with the ball uses his heel to send the ball to his teammate.

73

LONG BALL ON GROUND
Use the power of the instep to cover a lot of ground in one pass

At times you'll want your team to sacrifice some accuracy for distance. If a player can send the ball across the field to a wide-open player, you might get a breakaway. In this instance, the inside or outside of the foot will never create the power that a player needs to get that ball all the way across the field.

The way to get power in a pass is to use the instep to propel the ball. It's the hardest part of the foot. Show your players where the instep is. Have them all touch it for you. It's important that they understand that they're supposed to use this part of the foot to kick because they will naturally choose the toe otherwise.

Steering the toe-kickers toward the instep will be one of the hardest things you'll have to do as a coach. The kids are going to be far more successful initially if they use their toes, and they will not grasp the concept of long-term gain.

The Planting Foot

- Making a successful long pass isn't a matter of just switching to a different part of the foot. There are a number of other steps a player should take.

- The nonkicking foot is called the "planting foot." As the player approaches the

ball for a kick, she should place her planting foot about 3 inches from the ball.

- If she wants to keep the ball on the ground, the planting foot should be roughly even with the ball.

The Instep

- When a player needs to make a long, strong pass, she should use the instep.

- The instep is the hard, bony part of the foot located on top of the foot. Some coaches like to refer to it

as the "shoelace" part of the foot in order to make it clearer to young kids.

- The toe should be kept pointed. It should never be used for the kick itself.

KNACK COACHING YOUTH SOCCER

(Sometimes it will be hard for a coach as well to accept the concept of long-term gain!)

No matter how much time you spend working on the long, lofted kick, you're going to find that some players will just naturally be better at it than others. THese players should take the bulk of your goal kicks, corner kicks, and direct kicks. For instance, the goal kick needs to clear the 18 before anyone can touch it. It's a matter of necessity to use your biggest kicker. Explain to the team that each player has a role to play.

Contact

- When contacting the ball, the player should approach at a slight angle.

- Instead of keeping the leg rigid, the way a player might in a short push pass, the leg moves at all joints.

- The leg swings back at the hip, knee, and ankle. The body moves forward. Just before contact, the leg swings forward, and the knee and the ankle snap.

- Contact on the ball should be right through the center.

Knee Placement and Follow-through

- To keep the ball on the ground, the knee should be over the ball. Placing the planting foot parallel to the ball will make this happen automatically.

- After kicking, the player should follow through with his kick. Not only his leg but also his body follow through. He should be moving forward.

- Some players can get their follow-throughs as high as chest level.

LONG BALL IN AIR
Lift the ball over the defense

A ball in the air is sometimes called a "50/50 ball." It's up for grabs for either team. As a result, this ball is not ideal for the game of Keep Away. The high lofted pass does, however, have some uses.

If you have some speed on your forward line and your team is on the attack, a lofted ball over the defense and into the open space can really pay off. Your strikers need to be ready to sprint forward the moment the ball is released. If they can outsprint the defenders, then they have a breakaway. The passer has to control his chip so that it doesn't go so far that the goalkeeper can come from the other direction and pick it up.

Lofted balls also come in handy to clear the ball away from the goal and down the sideline. Train your outside players to go wide whenever your team has possession. If the opponents have collapsed to the middle, the sidelines are wide

Planting the Foot

- When a player is trying to get a ball up into the air, he'll want to move his planting foot back a bit.

- It depends on the size of the kicker, but a player should look to plant his foot 8 to 10 inches back and a little off to the side.

- If the ball is going to be a shorter chip, then the planting foot should be closer.

- Again, the player should approach the ball at an angle, perhaps one even more severe.

Contact Underneath

- If you think of the ball as a globe, the contact point should be somewhere in the Southern Hemisphere—beneath the equator of the ball. In other words, the player should get his foot underneath the ball.

- If the foot is underneath the ball, the follow-through will naturally bring the leg upward in addition to forward.

- Contact should be in the center.

open. A pass along the ground will be intercepted by the opponents, but a ball lofted over their heads will reach the sideline safely.

Trouble with Lofting

- If a player is having trouble lofting the ball—and almost all of them will at first—you'll need to check both his knee and his planting foot.

- To loft the ball, the knee and the planting foot should both be behind the ball on contact.

- If the player is executing both of these moves correctly, then he's probably contacting the ball too high.

Trouble with Power

- If a player, on the other hand, can loft the ball but is having trouble getting any power behind it, the problem is most likely the follow-through.

- Be sure the player's leg snaps all the way through the kick and ends up high.

- The player's body should also be running through the whole kick.

DRILLS FOR 4- TO 6-YEAR-OLDS
Repetition, repetition, repetition

When you introduce a drill or a game, the children at this age are not going to grasp it right away. Don't get discouraged and scrap the drill. It's not the fault of the drill or your explanation. It's just a function of their age.

Keep repeating the drill for a few weeks. If you find that the children still are not grasping or enjoying the drill, then maybe it's a bad drill after all. But usually it's just taken a little bit of repetition to get the kids to have fun with it.

If you've ever watched a kid's show on television, you'll quickly understand that repetition is the primary tool for teaching children of this age. In fact, the most popular kid's show on television is a show that repeats the same episode throughout the week.

Because literally everything is new to kids in this world, they take great comfort in seeing the same thing repeated. It helps them learn that this is something that's going to be

Sink the Subs

- Set up cones all over the playing area. These are the subs.

- Two players are the submarine commanders. They don't have a ball. All other players have a ball.

- The players with the balls pass their balls to the cones, trying to knock the cones over by hitting them with the balls.

- The sub commanders race around putting the cones back up.

Soccer Golf

- This is a fun game if you're practicing in a park with some trees or other obstacles.

- Set up a nine-"hole" course, using trees, playground equipment, soccer goals, and so forth as the holes.

- Players have to pass the ball and hit the "hole."

- They can't move on to the next hole until they've hit the first one.

consistently true in life, and it's also comforting for them to feel that they've mastered something.

So whether it's a song or the alphabet or a soccer drill, children like to see it repeated. This fact doesn't mean that you should dwell on one particular game or drill in practice. Quite the opposite, in fact. The kids will be bored and lose focus quickly if you don't change things up. The key, rather, is to bring the same drills back each practice.

To make a drill competitive, you can have it be a race or count how many passes it takes the players to complete the course.

Passing Relay

- Divide the players into two or three teams and line them up about 10 feet apart from each other, with the first player starting on the end line.

- Now give each end line player a ball. The players must pass the ball down their line to the end and back.

- The first team to get its ball back is the winner.

Ouch!

- In this drill all players have a ball.

- You jog around in the box, and the players try to kick their balls and hit you.

- The players get a point each time they hit you. You should yell "Ouch!" each time you are hit to make the game fun.

DRILLS FOR 7- TO 10-YEAR-OLDS

Be sure players are committed to proper technique, even when they're playing a game

Every game or drill presents its own challenge to a coach. Some are more complicated, so you have to instruct the players where to go throughout the drill. Some require you to keep score. Some force you to focus on the boundaries, lest someone lose the ball or step out. Some force you even to bark like a dog.

But regardless of what unusual focus you may need for a particular drill, you can't lose sight of the basics. You're out on the field to teach your players how to play soccer, and you're using a particular drill to teach them a particular skill. Make sure they're actually using it.

For instance, seven-year-olds find that they get much more

Short, Short, Long

- Divide the players into groups of three, one ball for each group.

- Players should line up with about 10 feet in between. One of the end players starts with the ball.

- The end player passes a short pass to the middle player. He controls it, turns, and makes a short pass back. That player makes a long pass to the far player, who then begins the drill again from his side.

- Stress accuracy in this drill.

Cannonball Run

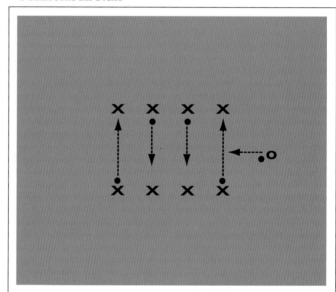

- Divide the players into two teams.

- The players on one team will be the cannons, and the others will be the targets.

- The cannons line up in two rows across from each other, one ball for each pair.

- The targets have to dribble their balls through this "alley" of cannons without themselves or their balls being hit. If they're hit, they're out.

- Then have them switch places.

power from kicking with their toes than with their insteps. They may lapse into that practice just to be more successful at whatever game you're playing. Don't let that happen.

And just because a drill focuses on one skill doesn't mean you should let the other skills slide. Always insist that your players use the proper technique every time they touch the ball.

Line Drill

- Divide the players into groups of three. Each group should have a ball. Players should be about 10 yards apart.

- The ball starts with the player in the middle. The player passes the ball to one of the end players and takes the end player's place.

- That player controls the ball and passes to the other end player, moving forward and taking his place.

- Players continue exchanging places.

Give and Go

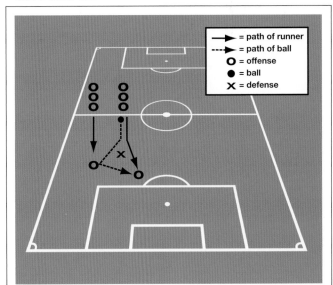

→ = path of runner
---→ = path of ball
○ = offense
● = ball
X = defense

- Divide the players into two lines. One line has the balls.

- You are the defender to start (players can take this position later after the kids get the hang of the drill).

- The player dribbles forward, and the first player in the other line moves forward, too.

- When the defender challenges, he passes the ball to his teammate and sprints around the defender.

- The teammate passes the ball back on the other side of the defender.

81

DRILLS FOR 11- TO 14-YEAR-OLDS

Fewer drills but longer focus improve teaching at this level

Along with the growing maturity, you have the growing attention span. You as coach still have to play the role of entertainer, but the bits don't have to be so small.

When you plan your practices, you can now have fewer drills. You can also have more complicated drills that might take a little longer to explain. Then, after the explanation part is done and the players are actually doing the drill, you can have them stay with it for much longer. They may not be thrilled with the longer time on a boring drill, but they will be perfectly happy with the longer time when they're doing a drill they love. Because of this fact, you have to make sure you mix it up.

Just remember to end on a high note. You want the kids to head home thinking about how much fun they had at practice. If you end with a painful sprinting exercise, you can be certain they'll be having different thoughts.

Passing for Points

- Divide the players into two teams.

- To emphasize the importance of passing, take away the focus on scoring goals. Play a full-field game but have no goals.

- A team gets a point only if it makes three consecutive passes to a teammate, without the other team getting control of the ball.

- After the players get good at this, you can increase the goal to five consecutive passes.

The Weave

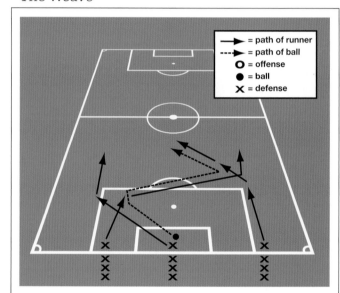

= path of runner
= path of ball
O = offense
● = ball
X = defense

- Divide the players into three lines. The balls should all be in the center line.

- The first player in the middle line passes either left or right—leading the player with the ball—and then runs behind that player to take his spot on the wing.

- The player receiving the ball runs to the middle to meet it and then passes to the third player. He then runs behind the third player and so on.

- The players weave down the field, learning to both meet the ball and move to the open space.

Having three teams (rather than two) work best for this drill because it makes the team think about not only offense and defense but also about changing the direction of the ball. Having more teams doesn't work because you don't want kids sitting out for a long period of time.

Three-cone Drill

- Divide the players into three even teams. Each team will have a triangular goal, made up of cones each about 3 feet apart. Each team has a ball to start the game.

- The object of the game is to knock down the opponents' cones.

- Players pass, dribble, and shoot at the cones.

- A team is out when all three cones are knocked over.

3 versus 2 versus 1

- Three players start the drill by moving the ball toward the goal. Two defenders try to stop them from scoring. This is the "3 versus 2" part.

- When a defender steals the ball or a goal is scored, the two defenders turn into offensive players. The person who lost the ball (or scored the goal) races back to become a defender, trying to prevent the other two from shooting on the other goal. This is the "2 versus 1" part.

- The other two players remain behind to become the next two new defenders for a new group of three.

FINESSE SHOTS

An accurate pass close to the goal often is the most effective shot

When people picture a shot on a soccer goal, most envision a powerful shot arcing high into the corner or a bullet flying just out of reach of the keeper's fingertips. The truth of the matter is that just as many goals are scored by perfectly placed soft shots, when the defense has been pulled out of position and an attacker finds herself with the ball in front of a gap in the goal. These are called "finesse shots."

A finesse shot should be a simple, accurate pass with the in-

side of the foot—the most accurate way to distribute the ball. Although it seems simple, it's astounding how many times a player in close range blows an easy shot. He might wind up for a power shot that just goes right over the goal, or he might panic and just bump it straight to the keeper. Coaches should make finesse shots part of their regular practicing.

Accuracy

- When a player is right in front of the goal, accuracy is important. He doesn't need power because the ball isn't going far.

- A player needs to focus on the ability to place the

ball just out of reach of the keeper.

- Therefore, when a player takes this shot, he should use the inside of his foot to ensure accuracy.

Finding the Spot

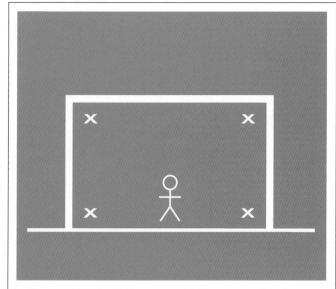

- Finesse shots should be placed in the corners of the goal.

- The ball will tend to go where the player is looking. Most players look at the goalkeeper.

- It is important for players to practice looking at the corners of the goal while shooting, so their shots will go there.

- Squaring up to one of the corners will help.

The players on the far side frequently won't be marked as tightly as the ones nearer to the ball. A player might find himself unguarded with a quick sprint to the goal

The Set-up

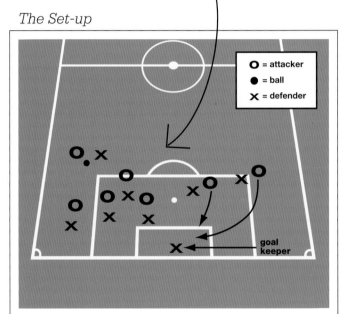

O = attacker
● = ball
X = defender

goal keeper

- Most finesse shots will come from a cross situation. The ball has been on one side of the field, so the keeper has shifted over to cut off the angle.

- Teach your far-side players to crash the goal in this situation—paying attention to the offsides rule, of course.

- Then they'll be in position to tap the ball into the goal after a cross.

Garbage Goal

- Many goals are scored when there is a scramble in the box or the keeper drops the ball.

- No fancy shooting is necessary in this case. A quick reaction and a foot on the ball will frequently result in a goal.

- This is one more reason why following the shot is important. This applies to not only the shooter but also to all forwards.

FINISHING

DRILLS FOR 4- TO 6-YEAR-OLDS
Play up the silly role to increase participation

When you're coaching preschoolers and kindergarteners, you're always going to have reluctant participants. They might miss Mom, or they might not have any concept of competition, they may not "get" the appeal of kicking a ball around the field, or they simply might be distracted by a dandelion.

This is okay. Don't expect instant success with everyone. One way to encourage participation and fun is to focus on the kids who are doing the drill and enjoying it. Be positive with your comments. Don't focus on the kids who are not engaged. Oftentimes the kids who are not engaged might be apprehensive about the whole soccer program, but in their own time they'll be participating as long as it looks like it's fun to do so.

Keep the practices fun and silly, and you'll draw in more and more kids each time. And don't minimize the importance

Square Soccer

- Divide the players into two teams. Set up four cones in a small square—the bigger the team, the bigger the square.

- Each team defends two adjacent sides of the square, while at the same time they try to shoot the ball over the opponent's side.

- Players must not let the ball go over their lines, and players are not allowed into the center of the square.

- Add more balls to make it more challenging.

Follow the Shot

- To teach kids to follow their shots, have them run into the goal to retrieve their ball after shooting.

- If you have them just shoot and go back in line, they'll get into bad habits (not to mention make more work for you).

- Turn this practice into a game by having two players go at once, battle it out to take the shot, and then battle it out again to retrieve the ball.

of silly at this age. It might be hard for you to do this, but when you're a pirate, you have to embrace the role, accent and all. When you're a bulldog, you have to growl and bark ferociously. It makes all the difference with children of this age. They'll rush to participate, and then they'll learn without being aware of it.

Two versus Two

- The best way to teach young players how to play soccer is to set up a minigame. Two against two is perfect at this level.

- Divide the players into groups of four and set up two goals, not too far away from each other, for each foursome.

- Now have them play a two-on-two game.

- By not having to fight the big swarm around the ball that they'd get with a larger group, they gain a stronger sense of the game.

Scoring on the Coach

- For this drill you should be on your knees in the goal. Players are in a line starting at around the penalty mark. They have the balls.

- One at a time players try to score. They can take one dribble, and then they must shoot.

- Remember that at this age players love to score, but they must think that you're actually trying to make the save.

DRILLS FOR 7- TO 10-YEAR-OLDS
Take shooting skills up a notch to take advantage of the big goal

Kids in this age range have probably been shooting on goals for a while, but their goals might be small nets on the ground or even just cones. Every move up to a higher level is going to bring a bigger goal right along with it. This is a challenge for the goalkeeper at this level, but it creates many more opportunities for enterprising shooters.

Your coaching goal at this level will be to take your players' shooting skills up a notch. Nine- and ten-year-olds will most

definitely be playing with a regulation-size goal, as will many seven- and eight-year-olds. Some leagues for seven- and eight-year-olds will have them playing with smaller goals, but nonetheless, they certainly won't be cones on the ground.

Your shooters need to be able to take advantage of the increased goal size. It's a big goal, but the goalkeeper will still be pretty tiny. Teach your players to go for the corners. This is a great habit to get them into early. Also, if all your players

Half Volley

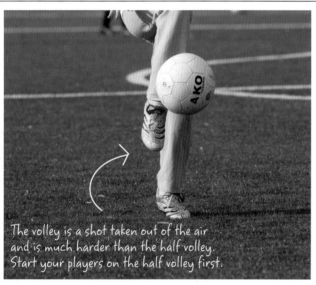

The volley is a shot taken out of the air and is much harder than the half volley. Start your players on the half volley first.

- Until now your players have taken their shots with a ball that's always on the ground. Now you need them to practice taking a bouncing ball and turning it into a shot.

- Start by having them drop the ball in front of them.

The second it bounces, they should try to kick it toward the goal. This is called a "half volley."

- Timing is the hardest part of this drill.

Wall Shots

- It's important to get the players thinking about shooting into the corners of the goal, so the key is eliminating the middle area as a shot option.

- On a wall tape off a regulation-sized goal and tape off the middle area.

- Line the players up in front

and have them take shots. They get one point for getting the ball to the edges, and they lose a point if they hit the middle.

- Have the players shout out their points before they shoot. The player with the most points at the end is the winner.

keep their shots rolling along the ground, then they won't be taking advantage of the short goalkeeper. With each year, the keeper grows, but the goal stays the same. Now is the time to help your players work on getting their shots up into the air.

Rotate in players to be the goalkeeper so that each learns the tough spots to handle.

Cones in the Corners

- If you don't have a wall, an easy way to eliminate the middle is to put two cones, each 3 or 4 feet from the goal posts.

- Players have to get the ball between the cones and the goal posts in order for it to count.

- Again, they lose a point for balls in the middle area.

One on One

- Having a player actually be the goalkeeper is a great way to show him what shots are the toughest to handle.

- Have one player be the shooter and one player be the keeper. Have them take ten shots and then switch places. Keep score.

- You'll have to mark off some sort of boundary line, so the shooter doesn't get in too close.

DRILLS FOR 11- TO 14-YEAR-OLDS
Practice a variety of shots to increase the chances of scoring

After players reach the older ages, their shots can get even more sophisticated. They can shoot from farther out, they can one-touch a ball into the goal, and they can try to add spin to their lofted balls. They also can start using their heads to manipulate the ball, and a head shot in front of the goal can be a powerful scoring weapon.

One of the other shots they're going to start working on is the volley shot. Volleys are shots that are taken while the ball is in the air. Balls will be crossed into the box or be bouncing off heads. There's no time to settle the ball on the ground, so the shot will need to be taken in the air. Volleys are always taken with the instep. Some might be a straight shot. Others will be a side volley, in which the player swings his leg around to connect with the ball.

Another way to expand your players' repertoire of shots is to teach them to connect with the ball slightly off center. Doing

Power and Header

- Now the players are old enough to shoot with their head. Stand on the side of the goal with all the balls. Line the players up at the 18.

- Roll a ball to the first player. She takes a shot and then comes in close to receive a second airborne ball that she shoots with her head.

- If she makes one of the two shots, she goes back into the line. If she misses both, she's out and helps you retrieve the balls.

Wall with X's

- Again, the wall can be used to help players target their shots. This time you want to make it even more specific by placing X's at various spots in the goal.

- Have the kids take turns shooting and keep their scores. Go through the line three or four times.

- After you've gone through the drill with the right foot, repeat it with the left foot.

- The player with the top score wins.

this will give the ball a little spin and allow it to "bend" as it arcs through the air.

You should also make your players focus on taking shots with their left foot. Hopefully, for a long time you've been running drills that focus on using both feet, but even if you've done this religiously your players will still be reluctant. Now you have to insist. You can even give double points for a goal scored with the left foot (unless it's by a lefty) during practice.

Make sure you do not include defense for this drill, at least initially. You want you players to grasp the concept of immediately turning a cross into a goal.

Volley Kick

- You can also use a wall to have your players practice volley kicks, but if you don't have a wall, then pair your players up.

- Start simply by having them drop the ball out of their hands and kick the ball

before it hits the ground. Doing this will get them used to how it feels.

- Then they need to learn timing, so they should try to volley the ball as it comes back from the wall or the other player.

Crossing Shot

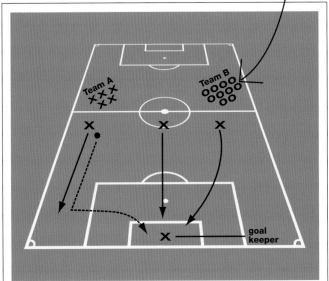

- Divide the players into two teams. Three players from each team go at once. A goalkeeper is in goal against both teams.

- One player from Team A crosses the ball into his two other teammates.

- They try to score. If they

score off their head, it's five points, a volley is three points, and if they control and shoot, it's one point.

- Now three players from Team B go.

- At the end of five minutes, the team with the most points wins.

GAMES FOR ALL
Games are a great teaching tool, but follow sound principles

The list of advantages of playing games during soccer practice goes on forever. Very few coaches don't use this teaching method to keep players on the team and coming to practice. But are there any disadvantages?

If a coach uses too many games that are only loosely tied into soccer skills, he can waste a lot of valuable practice time. Some of the games listed in this book are ideal for the youngest children but really aren't valuable when used with the older players, as much as those kids might enjoy them. That doesn't mean you can't throw in an old favorite every now and then—just don't make it a centerpiece of every practice.

Another disadvantage is that a lot of games keep eliminating players until there is one winner left. This adds a little competition and challenge, but it also means that you'll have kids sitting out doing nothing. You can require that players

KNACK COACHING YOUTH SOCCER

World Cup

You can help the players come up with other countries if there are duplicates.

- Divide players into pairs. Members of each pair decide which country they represent. This game is played inside the 18 with a goalkeeper playing against all the teams.

- You throw out three balls, and teams try to score. When they shoot, they must call out their country's name.

- If they score, they're out. The last team remaining sits out the next round.

- To protect the keeper, players are not allowed to shoot inside the 6.

Goalie Game

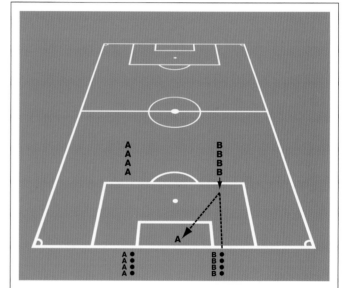

- Divide players into two teams, one on either side of the goal. Each puts half its players on the 18 and half on the end line with the balls.

- Team A puts one of its players in the goal. Team B passes the ball from the goal line to the first player in line on the 18. That player takes a shot without controlling the ball.

- The shooter becomes the goalie. Team A now passes the ball.

- After all players take a shot, the team with the most goals wins.

94

who are eliminated must juggle on the sideline, but it's still not ideal.

Unfortunately, the other complication is that the kids who need the most help and skill repetition are usually the ones who are eliminated first. They should be the ones staying in the drill, while the more experienced and skilled players sit out.

One way to rectify this situation is to have someone just sit out one round. He goes back into the game when he's replaced or a new round has started.

This game can also be played against a all or between two cones of short distance. If you are playing with a regular goal with a keeper, you should force the players to shoot outside of the 18.

Knock Out

- Line up your players in front of the goal, and put in a goalkeeper.

- Player 1 shoots from somewhere outside of the 18. If she scores, she goes to the end of the line. If Player 1 misses, however, she retrieves her ball and keeps shooting until she scores.

- If the keeper stops it, she should throw it back at for Player 1 to shoot again.

- The next person in line shoots with the second ball. If Player 2 scores first, Player 1 is out. If Player 1 scores first she goes to the end of the line and Player 3 comes in to try to knock out Player 2.

Power and Finesse

- You should be on one side of the goal with all the balls. Line up the players at the 18.

- Roll a ball to the first player. He takes a power shot and then comes in close to receive a second ball, which must be a finesse shot to the corner.

- If he makes one of the two shots, he goes back into the line. If he misses both, he's out and helps you retrieve the balls.

- If he makes both shots, he picks out another player, who now also has to make both shots to stay in the game.

95

MECHANICS

Teach players to connect with the forehead because a face ball hurts

By the time players are eleven or twelve, their bodies are strong enough and developed enough to add heading to their game. Heading the ball is an extremely valuable skill for any soccer player, and the sooner your players can join the head game, the better.

Unfortunately, your players may be much more reluctant than you are. Because it's not safe for them to start heading the ball at a young age, they're not in the habit. In addition,

many players are afraid that a head ball is going to hurt. And, of course, sometimes it does—especially when they're first learning.

So, with that in mind, you want to start them off gently. If you have a ball on a rope, you can suspend it from a tree and have your players practice heading. This device allows them to practice contact points and body snaps in a nonpainful manner. In addition, they can do it repeatedly without hav-

Contact Point

- It's important that you make it very clear to your players that every head ball will use the forehead as the contact point, no matter which direction a player wants to send the ball.

- To get kids used to doing this, have them hold the

ball above their head and drop it onto their forehead.

- Now have them toss the ball up a little to force them to move a little.

- Finally, begin soft tosses.

Ready Position

- Players square their body to the ball, their knees bent, ready to jump.

- The arm position is a matter of personal preference: out for balance, back for jumping momentum, or up as if they were going to catch the ball.

- When the ball comes in, the player needs to lock his neck and head in place. The snap that gives the header power needs to come from his body.

- A player's eyes should be tracking the ball. Be sure the player watches the ball the whole way in.

ing to run after the ball. After they've mastered this drill, you can raise the rope to have them jump up to head the ball. Finally, raise the ball a bit more and have players run and jump up to it.

If you don't have a ball on a rope, then you're going to have to use soft toss. It's better if you are the feeder so that you can correct anything that might be wrong with the mechanics right off the bat. If you train the kids with good form in the soft toss, then they'll hopefully carry it over to more difficult feeds.

Snap Forward

- The power to hit a head ball should come from the stomach and back muscles.

- The head ball should never be from a neck snap.

- The player needs to arch his back and snap his body forward as one unit.

Jumping

- Unless a player is diving for a head ball, virtually all the headers he'll make involve heading while jumping up into the air.

- The players should jump first and then snap while they're in the air.

- After your players get used to basic heading mechanics, all the heading drills they do should be jump headers, but it's important to have the basics first. They should be second nature so that players can concentrate on timing their headers.

HEADING

CHOOSING THE DIRECTION

Use the head to send the ball forward, backward, and sideways

If the ball is kicked or thrown by your team, your players are not going to want to head the ball straight on. Doing that will just send the ball right back where it started from and much closer to your goal. Instead, they are going to have to learn how to redirect the ball.

A backwards header can continue a ball's forward momentum. Picture a scenario in front of the goal. A player on your team has taken a shot on goal from outside the 18. The keeper is coming out to grab it, but just before he does, another of your players jumps up and bumps the ball a little with his forehead. The ball doesn't change direction at all, but the bump might be enough to throw off the keeper's timing or, in an ideal situation, enough to bump the ball over the keeper entirely.

Headers to the side can be just as effective. These headers can be used at any part of the field. They aren't reserved for

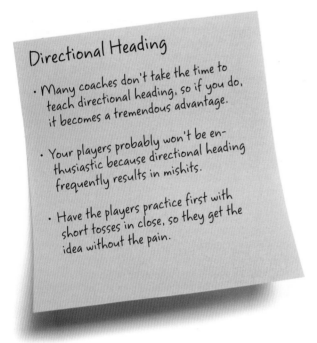

Directional Heading

- Many coaches don't take the time to teach directional heading, so if you do, it becomes a tremendous advantage.

- Your players probably won't be enthusiastic because directional heading frequently results in mishits.

- Have the players practice first with short tosses in close, so they get the idea without the pain.

Forward Heading

- This is the easiest type of heading and the one that's described in the mechanics.

- Your players will get the most power and most distance from a forward heading.

- Be sure your players master basic heading before you teach them to send the ball in another direction.

just the goal area. Don't expect your players to be good at heading right away or perhaps even for the entire time you have them under your influence. Because heading must start with older kids due to safety reasons, this is an entirely new skill for them. It's not until high school and college where heading becomes a factor. Nonethless, the more you encourage it and practice it, the more likely you are to see it in a game

Sideways Heading

- Moving the ball to the left or the right can throw the defense off, especially if the ball is coming out of the air—the defense doesn't expect the ball to do anything but go forward.

- The player should contact the ball with the forehead, but instead of snapping the whole body, it's more of a flick.

- This shot is especially effective as a give-and-go move. The player should head the ball to a teammate, then sprint forward, leaving his defender wondering where the head ball went.

Backward Heading

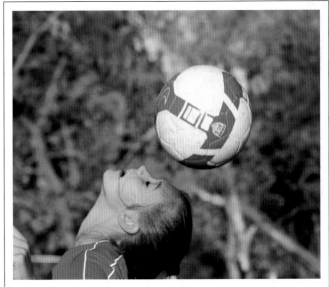

- Heading the ball backward can be a great way to have it continue forward.

- To head the ball backward, a player will still use the forehead to contact the ball.

- The player just touches the ball lightly, giving it a little boost but not redirecting the flight path of the ball.

- The backwards header is effective if a player knows he has a defender on his back. The little touch on the forehead is just enough to pop the ball up and over the defender.

DIVING HEADERS
Score a goal in the most exciting way possible

A diving header isn't used very often, but it's very exciting when a player does take his life in his hands, going after a low ball with his head. This is the stuff of the nightly news highlights and spectacular photos. You should probably teach this to some of your players, but don't be surprised if their parents aren't thrilled.

Not surprisingly, many of the mechanics are the same as a regular header. The player needs to be poised to spring—this time horizontally rather than vertically. The neck needs to remain locked. The contact point is the forehead and nowhere else. And, of course, timing is everything.

Diving headers are used to redirect a low ball into the goal. They are used in front of the goal and nowhere else on the field primarily because it is dangerous for a player to place his head at the level of everyone else's feet. Doing so seems worth it only in front of the goal.

Choose Your Divers Carefully

- The players who fight for every ball

- The players who are frequently on the ground

- The players who have already mastered heading

Ready Position

It's also important for the player to fling the arms forward to cushion her fall and avoid a face plant!

- The player should bend his knees, just as in a regular header, but this time he needs to get even lower, almost into a crouch.

- The player should square up to the ball.

- Arms should be back, ready to be flung forward to give his dive extra momentum.

And if you thought regular headers were unlikely to happen with your team, you can be sure that the chance of a diving header is even smaller. Nonetheless, you'll want to teach it at least once; you never know when you might find that kid who takes every opportunity to dive on the ground.

····· · · · YELLOW ● LIGHT · · · · ·····

Not every player has the mentality to be a diver. Rather than waste a lot of practice time teaching something that might be useless to many of your players, save it for a select few. You can offer it after practice for those who are interested.

Dive

- The dive should be parallel to the ground, not into it.

- You can have your players practice the dive by starting in a push-up position, albeit with the knees bent, ready to spring.

- Have your players first dive without the ball, so they will get used to that.

- Now give them a soft-toss ball that they dive into. Doing this gets them used to the motion without the bigger impact that a dive from a standing position would create.

Contacting the Ball

- As always, the contact should be on the forehead.

- Players should keep the neck locked.

- Eyes should be open, watching the ball the entire way, but the mouth should be closed. No one needs a mouth full of dirt to show for his or her efforts.

HEADING

101

STRATEGY

Teach your players to use their heads when they use their heads

After the head ball is introduced into the soccer game, the team that employs it will have a huge advantage. Every 50/50 ball can be gotten with the head before anyone can get it with a foot, chest, or thigh.

In addition, the goalkeeper's advantage in front of the goal is diminished a little because he can no longer wait until the ball reaches his chest level. Adding heading to the mix forces him to reach up and grab the ball high before an opponent's head gets on it. The high catch is less of a sure thing, and a header might even lead the keeper to choose to punch or tip the ball rather than catch it. No matter what, it changes the game and gives the heading team an edge.

Headers can be effective on the defensive side as well. Getting to a ball first is critical in front of the goal, so you should make sure you have some aggressive players who are willing to head the ball hard.

Power Shots

- The power head shot can be used to either defend a goal or to shoot at a goal.

- If a player is defending, the header should be a high clear out of the box.

- A power head shot on goal will often come from corner kicks and direct kicks.

- If the header stands on the far side of the goal from the kick, he can get the most power because he'll be heading the ball almost completely forward into the goal.

50/50 Balls

- If the ball is in the air, a player may not have the luxury of waiting until it gets down to his foot.

- If a defender is on your players, have them jump up and get that ball out of the air with their head.

- If a player uses his head, he'll have an advantage, especially if the move hasn't occurred to the defender.

- The ball can be headed in a pass to another teammate, but it can also be a shot on goal.

········· YELLOW ● LIGHT ·········

Tell your players that the goalkeeper rules the box. If a keeper thinks he can catch the ball, a header needs to get out of the way fast. Usually the keeper will shout "Keeper" if he can get it or "Away" if he wants the header to take the ball and get it away from the goal.

Having height in your forward line will help when it comes to heading balls into the goal.

Heading for a Goal

- Teach your players to use their heads to go after all lofted balls in front of the goal.

- The keeper will be reaching high with his hands, so your player's only chance is to go high as well. He can't use his hands, but he can use his head.

- A tall forward is always helpful for this reason.

- Because the keeper will be going high, the shot should be low. Heading in front of the goal should be a low shot to the corner.

Head Gear

- Some players wear protective head gear. This is tight-fitting foam padding that encircles the forehead and temples.

- Many parents have their kids wear head gear to protect them from concussions and other head injuries.

- Head gear is controversial because some doctors believe it actually causes more injuries for two reasons. First, headgear shifts often when a player heads the ball. Second, players are less likely to use the correct technique because they feel invulnerable.

HEADING

HEADING DRILLS
Hone the heading skills without overdoing it

The problem with heading drills is the sensitivity factor. No matter how skilled players are with head balls, they still are going to feel some pain—if not an outright headache—after ten minutes or so of straight heading.

In addition, there's the safety factor. Coaches are told to keep their youngest players from heading. The necks and bodies of these players aren't strong enough or developed enough to withstand repeated blows to the head. It's like giving a player a bunch of miniconcussions. Even though your players might be old enough to begin heading, you don't want to overdo it and cause unnecessary damage.

That said, you will need to provide some instruction and do a limited amount of drilling, or else your team will be at a decided disadvantage.

Server and Header

- Divide your players into pairs, each with one ball. Have one player be the tosser and the other the header. They should stand 10–15 feet apart.

- The tosser should throw an easy soft ball to the header, who should practice proper technique and snap forward on contact. After a few minutes, the players should switch places.

- Next, take it up a notch by having the header jump before he contacts the ball.

- Finally, have the players move down the field, so they are heading on the move.

Add a Defender

- Divide the players into groups of three. Each group has one ball.

- This drill is the same as the previous one, but now the header has the added pressure of trying to head in competition.

- To start, don't have the defender try for the ball. He should jump and be an obstacle, but that's all.

- Now take it up a level by having the defender try to get the ball as well.

For all heading drills, players should make sure they toss the ball softly to their teammate.

Directing the Ball

- Divide the players into groups of three with one ball for each group.

- In this drill there's a tosser, a header, and a receiver. The receiver first stands to the right of the header. When the ball is tossed, the header tries to direct the ball to the receiver. The receiver returns the ball to the tosser.

- Next, the receiver moves behind the header, so the header has to go backward.

- Finally, the header moves to the left side. After the three tosses, the players rotate positions.

Isolating the Body

- If players are having trouble getting the body snap, put them on their knees.

- Because they won't be able to use their legs to jump into the ball or give them power, they'll learn to use their bodies.

- Be sure they're keeping their necks rigid.

GAMES
Have fun with head ball games

Games that focus solely on heading the ball are few, but there are some you can use. You'll notice that some of them are similar to games that are used for other skills. Power and Header is similar to Power and Finesse.

If you find that your players like a specific game, see if it can be adapted for heading use. Not only will it save you explanation time, but also you'll know that your players will be excited to play it. They might not gripe so much about having to use their heads.

Although you need to practice heading, you should keep the heading games to a minimum. Do them for five to ten minutes tops. It's better to do a little at every practice than to spend a long time on heading at one practice.

Heading Relay

The last person in line runs up to be the feeder when the ball drops, so the players shift positions in line.

- Divide your players into two or three teams, each with five to seven players in it.

- Have the first player in line toss the ball to the next. He must then use a light backward header to get the ball to the next player in

line, who must immediately head it to the next, and so forth.

- You can have players do this drill until one team gets the ball all the way to the end of the line.

Juggling

- Juggling with the head helps players get comfortable contacting the ball with the forehead.

- Initially have your players juggle on their own. See how many times they can

keep the ball in the air using only their head.

- Now divide them into groups of five or six. Have them work together to keep the ball aloft, again using only their head.

Players go through a psychological cycle when it comes to heading. When they're first allowed to head, they're very excited. They're also fearless. Then somewhere along the line, they get a ball in the face, and their attitude changes. They hate to use their heads. Be strong. Forge ahead. Force them to play heading games.

Ideally, the other end player could then make a short head pass into the middle, and the players keep heading in this manner, but this is tricky.

Short, Short, Long

- Divide the players into groups of three, one ball for each group.

- Players should line up with about 5 feet in between. One of the end players starts with the ball.

- The end player tosses the ball to the middle player. He heads an easy ball back to the first player, who then tries to head a hard, longer pass to the other end player.

Directional Heading

- Set up two little goals made from cones off to the side.

- The first player in line gets on his knees. Toss him the ball. The player must try to head the ball into one of the two goals.

- A player gets a point for scoring a goal. He should

keep track of his own points throughout the drill.

- After all players have done this drill, move off to the side. Players first have to redirect the ball to the goal away from the feed, and then they have to head the second ball back toward the feed.

HEADING

CULTIVATING THE KEEPER
You can dress them up, but they tend to want to get dirty

By the time the ball gets to the goal, ten players on the field have failed to do their job. Nonetheless, it's ultimately the keeper's responsibility to keep the ball from going into the goal. Of course, the keeper has an advantage that the rest of the players don't: She can use her hands. It may sound obvious, but this is the primary lesson that coaches need to teach their keepers. They know they can use their hands, but sometimes they'll still try to kick the ball away. Get their hands onto the ball for better control.

Because of this need you want to direct your gutsiest players toward that position in the goal mouth. You want players who are going to love diving onto the ground and jumping into the fray. The keeper should be the player who wants to grab every ball near her. Give her the green light to step into the swarm—as long as he plans on coming out of it with hands safely clutching the ball.

Gloves

- Gloves are a must. Even the cheapest version provides the keeper with a better grip for catching the ball.

- The palms are made of latex foam. Some keepers spit on their gloves. The moisture makes the gloves stickier.

- Many expensive gloves have finger guards, which not only protect the fingers but also provide extra support for weak fingers—a problem frequently found in young keepers.

- No matter how much you plan to spend on goalie gloves, though, you must be sure they fit!

Shirts

- Keeper shirts can be short-sleeved, but most are long-sleeved; many provide padding in the elbow area.

- The keeper is required to have a shirt that differs in color from his team's and the opposing team's uniforms and the referee's shirts.

- Because the keeper has different rules and safeguards, everyone should know who is who on the field.

- Most keepers wear a brightly colored shirt, hoping that subconsciously the shooter's eye—and therefore the shot—will be drawn to the splash of color.

Most importantly, the keeper needs to be the boss of the goal box. In addition to having a gutsy player, you want to cultivate the bossy player with the big mouth. The keeper needs to take charge and direct the action. The keeper who hangs back, waiting to see where the ball goes and hoping someone else will clear it out, is going to be the keeper who watches the ball go into the goal.

Shorts

- Although long pants might offer more leg protection, keepers have the option of wearing shorts—by far the preferred choice in hot weather.

- Most goalkeepers prefer to have built-in padding in the hip area, but it's in no way required.

- Some players prefer to use regular shorts but wear spandex shorts underneath with the padding built into this under layer.

Pants

- The pants, like the shorts, can have padding in the hip area but also have more room for protective padding elsewhere, especially in the knees. Some pants offer even lower back padding.

- Wearing pants can also offer the keeper protection against abrasions that might occur when sliding or diving onto the ground.

- Frequently pants are chosen purely for the fact that they can keep the legs warm in cold weather.

GOALKEEPING

STOPPING A ROLLING BALL
How to move, where to stand, and the best way to scoop a ball

When kids first start playing soccer, every shot on goal will be a ball that's rolling on the ground, so it makes sense to teach keeper skills for that type of ball first. At the very youngest level, some leagues don't use goalkeepers. However, by age six or seven the goalkeeper position has been added, and it's the rare seven-year-old who can loft the ball with any regularity.

When players are older, they'll be getting shots of all va-

rieties, but they'll still have plenty of shots that roll along the ground. Coaches who have older players need to make sure that their keepers are not using sloppy techniques just because the ball is rolling. What may seem like an easy ball could easily take a bad hop and become a goal. Keepers need to focus on fundamentals no matter how experienced they are.

Without question, the most important factor for goalkeep-

Pinkies Together

- No matter what the shot looks like, the keeper wants to get her hands behind the ball.

- For shots rolling on the ground, tell the keeper to focus on keeping her pinkies together, palms out. Doing this creates a wall for the ball to run into.

- If the pinkies aren't together, there's too big a gap, and the force of the ball can easily push the ball through the keeper's hands.

- After the ball is secured, the keeper should scoop the ball into her chest and hug it.

Body behind the Ball

- The keeper's first thought should be to get her body behind the ball if at all possible.

- She should never be reaching to the side to grab a ball if she has the time to get fully behind it.

- A rolling ball is slower than a shot in the air, so the keeper has a little more time to react.

- In addition to getting her body behind the ball, she should use this time to go out and meet the ball.

ers is learning positioning. It doesn't matter whether they are just starting out or are very experienced, and it doesn't matter whether the shot is a hard bullet through the air or a slow dribbler on the ground. In every instance, the goalkeeper needs to get her body behind the ball.

The feet are the key. The keeper wants to move her feet to get her body into position. It's a safeguard against a bad catch. If the ball should somehow pop out of the keeper's hands, then at least her body is there to act as a backboard.

The Pickup

- Some coaches advocate a bent-knee pickup. When coaching the youngest players, telling them to put one knee on the ground is a good way to get them to focus on using their body to block the ball.

- As they age, players should realize that the knee doesn't actually need to go all the way down because doing so limits the keeper's mobility should the ball bounce away.

- Other keepers prefer a straight-leg pickup, making sure that their legs are together, forming a solid wall to block the ball.

Diving

- As a last desperate measure, the goalie will need to dive to save some balls. She should stay low, springing out at an angle toward the ball.

- The keeper should land on the hip and leg, not the stomach. Padded shorts let this be done with less pain.

- It's important for the keeper to make the catch first and not worry about the landing.

- After the catch is made, the keeper should hug the ball into her body.

111

GOALKEEPING

DEALING WITH A LOFTED BALL
Teach your keeper how to catch, tip, and punch that high shot on goal

Assuming that the ball is within reach, a shot on goal that is lofted into the air is actually a pretty easy shot for the keeper to handle. Nonetheless, it's important that your goalkeeper learn proper technique for catching the ball. You don't want to take any chances right in front of the goal. Many of the basics are similar to those for a rolling ball: The keeper should

stay focused, get her feet to the right spot, and get her body behind the ball.

If the ball is coming in too high for the keeper to make a solid catch, she can still make a difference as long as she can get a hand on it, deflecting it away from the goal. She can tip it over the cross bar if she's lucky. Or if the ball stays inbounds,

Ready Position

- If the play is down in front of the goal, the keeper needs to be about 1 foot off the goal line. She should be on the balls of her feet, ready to move left or right as the play on the field demands.

- Knees should be bent, prepared for a dive or a jump.

- Hands should be up, and elbows also should be bent. Now the arms are prepared to give with the force of the ball.

- Eyes are focused on the play at all times.

Making a W

- The keeper should create a *W* with her thumbs and forefingers to catch the ball.

- Doing this brings her hands close together, forming a solid wall for that hard shot. This way, even if she doesn't catch the ball, she's blocked it with her hands.

- If she catches the ball with her hands farther apart, there's more likelihood that the ball will slip through.

- After the keeper catches the ball, she wants to hug it to her body. No player is allowed to touch the keeper when she has possession of the ball.

sometimes that tip will give the goalkeeper a second chance to get her hand on it. Or the tip could be all the defense needs to get a foot on the ball and clear it out.

If the lofted ball is not right at the goal, a tip can be dangerous because the tip might send the ball into the goal. If the crowd is too dense for the keeper to make a clean save, she should take advantage of the fact that she alone can reach up above the crowd. If she can't grab the ball, she should try to punch it, using either a punch with one hand or a punch with her two fists together.

Tipping the Ball

- For a hard-to-catch ball near the top of the goal, the keeper should tip the shot over the crossbar.

- To practice, put balls into the goal and stand on the 6. The keeper grabs a ball and runs it out to you, handing it over. Then she backpedals to get back into place while

you toss the ball up high. She then tries to tap it over the cross bar.

- Reserve this drill for older players. The shots mostly roll on the ground for the youngest players, anyway, and you don't want them tipping it into the goal.

Punching the Ball

- The keeper can punch the ball with one hand or with the two hands together.

- It's important to punch the ball as far away from the goal area as possible, so again this is not a great alternative for the youngest kids.

- A drill for this skill would use one keeper and two or three headers standing in different spots.

- Toss the ball up near one of the headers, requiring the keeper to punch it out before the header can get his head on the ball.

GOALKEEPING

CUTTING THE ANGLE
Use the whole of the box by moving front to back and side to side

Positioning is everything for a goalkeeper, whether it's moving the body to get behind the ball when making a save or knowing where to stand when the play is out in front. Even if the action is away from the goal mouth at the other end of the field, the keeper has positioning responsibilities.

With the youngest players, don't be too focused on shifting in the goal. Just tell them to keep their eye on the ball and their bodies always facing toward the ball. That should be

plenty for them. As they get older you can show them how to shift side to side in the box.

The other significant movement that a keeper makes is moving out to the edges of the box. Again, this is just for the older kids. But if you are coaching older kids, you must make sure your keeper uses the entire goal box. When the action is at the other end of the field, she should move out to the edge of the 18. Now if the other team boots the ball to her

Moving in an Arc

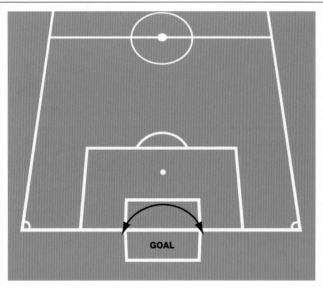

- The keeper should move in an arc across the goal.

- A keeper should always face a potential shot head on and be in the ready position.

- Train your keepers by having them do a side-to-side shuffle, following the arc back and forth in front of the goal.

Shifting

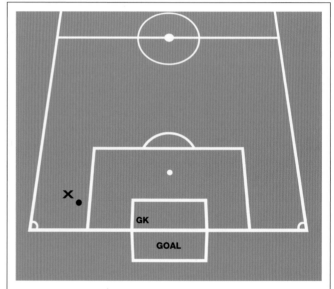

- If the ball comes toward the keeper from the side, he needs to shift to that side.

- The top priority is to prevent a goal at the near post. Although leaving part of the goal open is dangerous, it's best to leave the far side

open. It's a harder shot, and a teammate can defend that area.

- For a sharply angled shot, a keeper should be one arm's length away from the post so he can deflect it over the end line if he can't catch it.

end of the field, she doesn't have to race forward to be the first to get to it. This prevents a lot of breakaways.

········· YELLOW ●LIGHT ·········

For the youngest age levels, make sure the kids also know to stand 1 or 2 feet in front of the goal. Otherwise, you'll find some of them actually defending from inside the goal.

Moving Forward

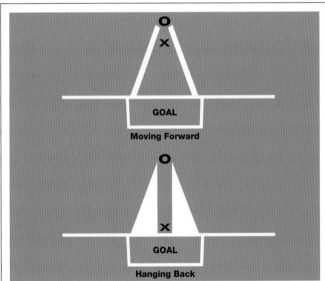

- If it's a one-on-one situation, the keeper is at a disadvantage, but if she hangs back, it's going to be worse.

- She needs to move forward to cut off the amount of open space in the box.

- Doing this also may force the shooter to take the shot too early or to dribble too far out in front.

- The keeper doesn't want to move in too quickly until she sees that the dribble gets too far out in front of the player.

Exiting the Box

- The keeper may come out of the box to get the ball if it appears that a forward might reach it before it rolls across the 18.

- If the keeper comes out, though, she automatically becomes a field player and may no longer use her hands to control the ball.

- Another time your keeper might use her foot is when the ball is specifically passed back to her from a teammate. In this instance, She is also not allowed to use her hands.

115

RELEASING THE BALL

Use punts, throws, and rollers to get the ball out to the team

Although catching the ball or saving the goal is a top priority for a keeper, it's only half of the equation. Now the keeper has to get rid of the ball and return it to play. Don't neglect this very important part of your keeper's education.

The rules give the keeper six seconds to release the ball. This is actually a fair amount of time, and you should encourage your keepers to take a deep breath and let their teammates move out of the box. Hopefully, the opponents will be moving away, too. Older kids should also be encouraged to use these six seconds to run the ball out to the edge of the box. The farther away from the goal, the better.

A keeper can use a number of types of releases. A goalkeeper can punt, which has the advantage of sending the ball far down the field. She can also roll or throw the ball out if he sees a player within reach. Doing this is much more accurate than punting. At the youngest levels, the keeper should al-

To the Side

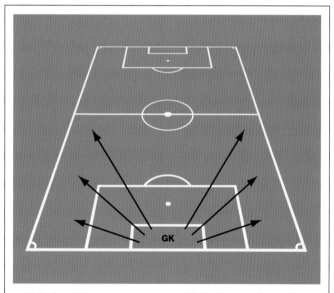

- Right from the start even the youngest keepers should be taught to send the ball out to the sideline.

- If a keeper sends the ball right out in front, and it is intercepted by the opponents, he then has to scram-ble back to get into place just as the ball is being shot, a recipe for a goal.

- The farther away the keeper is able to send the ball, the less he has to worry about angling it.

Punting

- If the keeper is going to punt, she should take the ball out to the 18.

- Keepers can try to punt to a specific teammate, but on a ball like that the other team will have plenty of time to move into position. The purpose of a punt is distance.

- Train your punters to take two or three steps before they punt the ball. If they're moving out to the 18-yard line, they're taking the steps anyway.

ways choose the rolling option. Not only is punting a skill the keeper probably doesn't have, but also rolling the ball out to a teammate avoids having the players try to get control of the ball out of the air.

If the opponents don't pull out, however, then they usually leave a player open closer to midfield, opening up the opportunity for a throw—much more dangerous for the opponents.

Rolling

- Rolling the ball is most common with all players.

- The youngest players really can't do anything else, and the oldest players recognize the value of maintaining possession over the value of kicking the ball far down the field.

- After the keeper saves the ball, she should take her allotted six seconds. If she slows the game down, most opponents will leave the goal box and wait for the ball to go back into play.

- Doing this usually opens up a defender for a nice, easy roll.

Throwing the Ball

- Keepers may throw the ball in any manner they choose, but most prefer a sidearm sling.

- Young players frequently try to replicate the throw-in from the sidelines. Make it clear to them that the keepers are not as restricted with their throws as the field players.

- A keeper should choose to throw when a teammate is wide open within reach.

WARM-UP DRILLS

Train the muscles and mind to get the body ready to stop the shots

Some teams have players who are solely keepers. Others have keepers who play on the field half the time and in the goal the other half. Either way, at some point the keepers need to warm up with exercises that are specifically designed to warm up the muscles and skills used in the goal.

If you have a keeper who also plays the field, then moving her in and out of the goal for drills during practice is fine. Assuming you'll scrimmage at the end, you can have the two

keepers throw the ball back and forth to each other just to get into the swing of things.

If, on the other hand, you have keepers who are solely keepers, you want to work with them a little more on their warm-up. If you have two keepers, you're in great shape. Have them work with each other. But if you have just one, then you should designate a different player each practice to spend time working with the keeper.

On the Knees

Real Shots

- Begin the warm-up with the keepers on their knees, rolling or throwing the ball back and forth. Doing this allows them to focus on good catching techniques without worrying about getting into position.

- Now have the players roll the ball to either side. Still

on her knees, the keeper will have to dive to the side to stop the ball. Doing this eases her into the standing dives that she'll do later in the game.

- If you don't have two keepers, designate a player to feed the keeper these balls.

- After the initial warm-up is complete, the feeder turns into a shooter. If you have two keepers, each should take about ten shots, then switch places.

- The shooter should give the keeper a variety of shots: high, low, hard, and slow dribblers to the corner.

- After the keeper's goal-saving skills are warmed up, work on timing for breakaways.

- The shooter should take a hard dribble from 25 yards out. The keeper will have to decide whether to charge in and grab the ball or stay back.

Before a game, keeper warm-up is critical for both younger and older players. The younger players need to get into the habit of using their hands to pick up the ball. The older players need to get their adrenaline pumping and get their bodies into diving mode. If you don't have two keepers, then designate a player to warm up the keeper. At the end of team warm-ups, the whole team can line up to shoot on the goal.

Doing this gives the keeper practice while training your field players to aggressively go after that air ball.

Punching and Tipping

- For older children it's important to practice shots that are just out of reach because there will be plenty of them. These are the shots that won't be caught.

- Players will have to punch, tip, or dive in order to save these goals.

- These balls should be done with a feeder rather than a shooter.

- Diving shots can be practiced from the push-up position first. Then have the keeper stand up and dive after shots from there.

Punting Drill

- Practices should also include punting and throwing to build both accuracy and strength.

- One fun punting drill is to have the players out within punting range (this will change based on the age and keeper's ability).

- The keeper has all the balls and punts them one at a time, calling out a player's name. That player must retrieve the ball before it hits the ground.

- If the player lets the ball bounce, he has to do a push-up.

119

KICKOFF
Start the game with an advantage and a plan

Coaches should not spend an enormous amount of time on kickoff plays. Such plays are not complicated, and there aren't a lot of options. Nonetheless, it is important for your team at least to have a plan. Every game starts with one team kicking off and the other team defending the kickoff. In the second half it's the opposite. So even if no goals are scored, every team will have one chance to kick off and one chance to defend it every game. It's important for coaches at least to discuss the kickoff briefly with their teams from both offensive and defensive perspectives.

From a defensive perspective, the aim is simple. After any forward movement of the ball, the defending team may enter the circle and go after it. However, until the ball is touched, the defending team is required to remain outside the center circle. The team should be ready to move on the kick and be ready to disrupt whatever plan the other team might have.

Two People

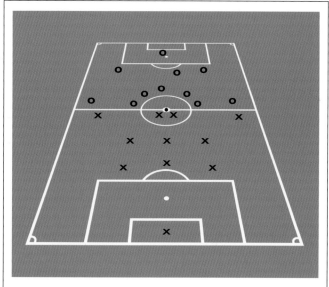

- The player who first touches the ball may not touch it again until another player has touched it.

- Many teams like to place two players right next to each other for the kickoff.

- If there's just one player at the kickoff, then his only option is a big kick forward.

- He can't pass the ball back because the ball has to go forward, and he can't dribble because another player must touch the ball first.

The First Touch

- With two players next to each other at the kickoff, the first touch will almost always be a small tap forward.

- The second player now takes charge. He may dribble, pass, or even shoot.

- He may go forward or backward or pass the ball back to the first player.

- Because the defending team will be charging into the middle, most teams like to get the ball out of the middle circle quickly.

Offensively there's a little more to the kickoff. The ball is placed in the center of the field, on the line. The first touch must move the ball forward, but this forward movement might be merely 1 inch. Here is where a team should have a plan, and it should be one that the whole team is aware of. Even though only a few players are involved in touching the ball in the kickoff, the rest of the team needs to be on the move and know what to expect.

The disadvantage here is that if the players lose possession, the ball is closer to their goal.

Going Forward

- One strategy is to send two players quickly down the sideline to receive a long kick out to the edges.

- The rest of the team needs to be aware that this is the plan so that the whole team rushes forward to support these two wing players.

- The advantage to this play is that it gets the ball quickly into the opponent's goal territory.

- The disadvantage is that most of the time your team loses possession immediately.

Going Backward

- Many teams like to pass the ball back to their center midfielder because doing so keeps the ball away from the defending team for just a little longer.

- Because maintaining possession is the aim of any team, these extra seconds will give a team a better assessment of its strategy.

- As the defending team rushes forward, the center midfielder will now either pass or dribble, and the game begins.

GOAL KICKS
Get the ball out of the box and still maintain possession

The goal kick is taken when the ball is kicked over the end line by the attacking team. To take the goal kick, the defending team may place the ball anywhere within the area marked off by the 6-yard line. Most coaches want their kickers to get the ball away from the goal and out to the sidelines.

Most goal kicks are taken by a strong kicker because you want to get the ball as far away from your goal as possible. However, you may want to throw in some short passes as well just to maintain possession. Keep mixing the kicks up to keep the other team off guard.

Although it is your kick, and you're transitioning into offense, your team still wants to mark up on the opponents because you're still in your defensive danger zone. Many players feel that the other team should be doing the marking and that they should be trying to get free, so you'll need to make the need clear to them.

On the Goal Box

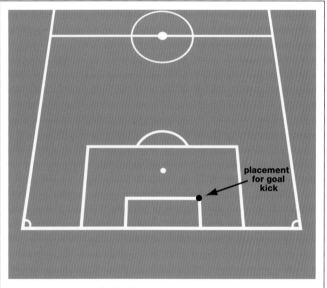

placement for goal kick

- Most teams put the ball on the actual 6-yard line, and they put it in the corner. Doing this gets the ball out as far as legally possible and as close to a sideline as possible.

- A team may put the ball in either corner. It doesn't matter which side the ball went out on.

- In fact, it can sometimes be strategically beneficial to switch sides if there's a dominant attacker on the other team or if play has been heavy on one side.

Big Kick

- One goal kick strategy is to clear the ball out of the danger zone. A long lofted kick out toward the sideline accomplishes this.

- Players should not kick this ball across in front of the goal.

- For this kick coaches should choose a strong kicker who is capable of consistently lofting the ball.

- Unfortunately, at the young ages when big kicks are the exception rather than the rule, the ball frequently gets turned right back over to the opponents.

The upside to this situation is that it gives the players very clear-cut instructions as to what to do. Many times the ball will be kicked, and players will just stand there. If they have to stay with an opponent and deny her the ball, then it gets all the players moving.

If yours is the offensive team, you want to put someone right on the 18 just in case of a missed kick. The younger the teams are, the more likely this is going to happen. Players have to make sure that they don't rush in and touch the ball too soon because the ball must clear the 18-yard line.

Short Kick

- Some teams opt to give a short pass out to an open defender on the side.

- This strategy is especially helpful, too, when you don't have a big kicker on your team.

- The advantage to this play is that the team maintains possession which would not happen with a long kick that turns into a 50/50 ball.

- The disadvantage is that opposing teams will quickly figure out your plan if this is your only option.

Attacking the Goal Kick

- Unless a team does a short kick to someone free on the side, the ball will be up for grabs as long as each team is doing its job.

- Place players right on the 18. Try to prevent the other team from gaining possession.

- You also want to load up on players on that side of the field.

123

CORNER KICKS FOR OFFENSE
Strategies for when your team is on the attack

Nearly half the goals scored in soccer come from set plays, and corner kicks are probably the most valuable opportunities because players are down in front of the goal. Added to that is the fact that both teams have a lot of players in the box. Your team is there to shoot, and the defense is there to mark up and clear the ball, but the result is a whole lot of confusion for the goalkeeper. Headers and garbage goals happen all the time off of corner kicks.

Ideally, the ball should be kicked so that it is in the air all the way to the far post of the goal. That situation presents the biggest challenge to the defending players because they don't know at what point and in which direction the ball will be going into the goal.

Some coaches like to devise a set play for their corner kicks. Some put all their players on the far part of the box, with some ready to move forward and others backward. Some like

In the Corner

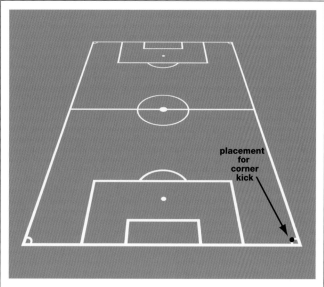

placement for corner kick

- Your corner kicker should be your player with the strongest foot.

- Your corner kicker should practice, figuring out which part of the corner arc he prefers. He needs to practice with the flag in place and from both sides of the field.

- The player in the corner should raise his hand right before his kick. This is a signal to his teammates to begin their moves.

Big Kick

- Some teams like to line up all of their players on the far post and then move in as the ball is kicked. Others like to start at the 18 and move in. Another strategy is just to spread out in the box.

- Whatever plan you have, your players need to be moving on the kick. They need to create confusion and motion, making it harder for the other team to defend against them.

- One player should always be coming in at the back post.

to line up players on the top of the penalty box before they make their runs. Others scatter players throughout the box with predetermined runs. Still others tell their players just to move and try to get open. The common denominator for all of these plays is that the attackers have to move when the ball is kicked. Their main job is trying to lose their defenders.

Usually the corner kicker will raise his hand, signaling the start of the kick. This is when the players begin their runs. If you have a consistent big kicker, you will have more options. If your kicker cannot get the ball to the goal mouth, then you will have to set up your players closer to the kick to fill the distance.

Short Kick	*On the Keeper*

- Occasionally you might want to try a short pass to a player near the corner. This player can then boot the ball into the middle. The fact that it's coming from a different direction might throw the defense off.

- This strategy is especially effective if you don't have a big kicker. Sometimes a ball in motion will go farther than a ball that is just sitting there.

- Unfortunately, this play can't be used every time or else the other team will catch on.

- Put one player on the keeper. Not only does doing this distract the keeper, but also it may make it harder for him to effectively catch the ball if you have a player who is jumping up to head it at the same time.

- It's unlikely that a player's head will ever be taller than a keeper's reach, but someone should be in there every time.

- If you have a tall player, move him into the box on a corner kick, even if he is a defender.

CORNER KICKS FOR DEFENSE

Where to stand and how to defend when the other team has the kick

A corner kick is one of the most dangerous moments for a defending team, especially if the opponents have someone with a big kick, so it's imperative that coaches teach their players how to defend against a corner kick. Philosophies vary as to whether a zone defense or a man-to-man defense is best, and many teams try a combination of both. Your job is to pick a philosophy and then impart it to your team.

Regardless of whether the defense is man-to-man or zone, the defenders should focus on clearing the ball and moving out of the danger zone as quickly as possible. Not only do your players want to get the ball away from their goal, but also you want to get your defenders out of there. If the ball does happen to come back in, they might catch a lazy attacker in an offsides trap. Initially, a player can't be offsides on the corner kick because the ball is on the end line, but after the ball is touched by someone else, this condition changes. If

Defending the Short Pass

- Some teams try to make a short pass, so you want to have a player out near the kicker, about 15 yards away.

- Not only does doing this take away the short pass option, but also it puts a player in place in the event that the kicker flubs the kick.

- With a successful long ball kick, this defender now marks up with the kicker.

Players on the Posts

- Many teams place a player on each post. These players are not marking up a specific player but rather are defending the area.

- The front post player does his best to block any low ball from crossing in front of the goal.

- The back post player is there for two reasons: If the keeper goes out to get the ball, he becomes the keeper's backup, or if the kick is crossed beyond the goal, he becomes the front post.

- Ultimately, however, the goalkeeper is in charge.

the defense pulls out, and an attacker stays behind, he might be offsides.

Another reason to clear the defenders out with the ball is that the other team might have overloaded the box for the corner kick. In this case, the more attackers you can spring free, the bigger advantage you might have.

Marking Up

- In a man-to-man defense or a combination man-to-man and zone defense, every attacker should be covered by a defender. This defender must stick with his attacker through the entire play.

- If you need to bring in some of your offense so that everyone is marked up, you should do that.

- The defender should place himself between the attacker and the goal.

Goalkeeper Responsibilities

- The goalkeeper has a lot of responsibilities anyway, but on a corner kick, her participation is vital.

- She needs to scan the field to see which player isn't marked and yell to some-one to take that unmarked player.

- She needs to shout "Keeper!" if she can get the kick or "Away!" if she can't, and she needs the defenders to get the ball away from the goal.

127

DIRECT & INDIRECT KICKS
Different strategies for one-touch and two-touch kicks

With direct and indirect kicks, much of the strategy depends on where on the field the kick is taken. If it's taken in front of the opponent's goal, the strategy is a little different than if it's taken in front of your own goal.

If the ball is in front of your own goal, then the strategy really should be similar to that of a goal kick. It's when the ball moves down the field that you might want to try something different. First of all, remember that the kicker doesn't have to wait for a whistle. One strategy might be to just jump and kick the ball to an open player before the defense has a chance to set up. Just remember that the ball must be completely stopped before it's restarted.

Most of the time, however, your team will want to take a shot on goal. And frequently the opponents will set up a wall to prevent this shot. If they do, they usually will try to get their wall in too close to the kick. If they do this, the kicker

Direct Kick

- If a kicker can consistently get the ball into the air, have him aim over the wall for either of the top two corners.

- Or have your team try a light chip over the wall and have your players run onto the ball for a header.

- Another option is to set up your attackers on the far side of the goal. The kicker should ignore the wall and the goal and instead cross the ball to these players.

- Or have your team try a quick short pass to a player.

The Wall

- If the kick is near the goal, your opponents will probably set up a wall. If they do, that doesn't mean that your team still can't shoot on the goal. Your team just has to shoot high.

- The other team may set up its wall too close.

- If it has too many defenders in the wall, a player is bound to be free. Your team should look for the pass.

should ask the referee to move the wall back. The coach is not allowed to ask that the wall be moved back. The kicker has to request it. A referee won't move the wall unless the kicker asks. If a kicker asks the referee to step in, then the kicker must wait for a whistle before he can kick the ball.

Indirect Kick

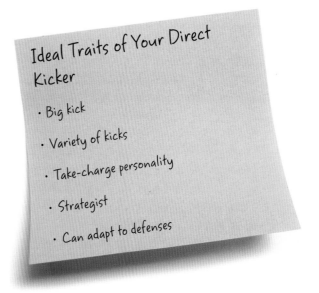

Ideal Traits of Your Direct Kicker

• Big kick

• Variety of kicks

• Take-charge personality

• Strategist

• Can adapt to defenses

- An indirect kick must touch at least two players before it goes into the goal; you need a strategy to handle this situation.

- One strategy is to have a player run over the ball. One player gives it a tap toward the real kicker. That kicker then takes a shot as if it were a direct kick.

- Another strategy is to run a give and go.

- A third strategy is to line the team up on the far side of the goal, send the ball over, and try for a head shot.

129

PENALTY KICK
What to do when a foul occurs in the box

A penalty kick is given when the defending team makes a direct kick foul inside the 18. If the foul results in an indirect kick, then that kick is taken just outside the 18. But if it's a foul that would have resulted in a direct kick, then the kick turns into a penalty kick.

Penalty kicks are an almost guaranteed goal for the team that's taking the kick. Roughly 85 percent of penalty kicks end up as goals. Nonetheless, that's assuming that the kick-ers are trained in how to take penalty kicks. At the younger levels, many more of the penalty kicks are saved—primarily because kids can't seem to kick the ball into the corner. They are drawn to the center of the goal.

As a coach, you don't want to spend an enormous amount of time training players for the penalty kick situation, but you do need to spend a little time on it for a few reasons:

It's an almost guaranteed goal, so your team cannot squan-

Preparing for the Kick

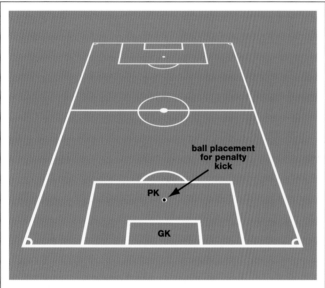

ball placement for penalty kick

PK

GK

- One player takes the kick. The coach may choose the kicker regardless of who is fouled.

- The goalkeeper must have both feet on the end line at the start of the kick.

- The ball is placed on the 12-yard hash mark and may not be moving at the start of the kick.

- The referee will ensure that both parties are ready and will then blow the whistle.

The Rest of the Team

- With the exception of the keeper and the shooter, the remainder of both teams must stand fully outside the 18.

- There is a small arc at the top of the box. Players must stand outside this arc as well—it completes the 10-foot radius around the ball.

- As soon as the kick is taken, the players are allowed to rush into the box to deal with any rebounding ball.

- The original kicker may not touch the ball until someone else has first.

der the opportunity. It's important to get familiar with it.

You get to choose who takes the penalty kick, so you want to know who your top kickers are.

Your goalkeeper has to know how to defend against the kick.

Even though the situation is just a kicker and a keeper, the other players should be aware of the rules and where to stand.

After you find your penalty shot takers (and have more than one), you can have them practice hitting the corners by set-ting up cones in each corner. Have them take ten shots each in both directions.

Keeper Strategies

- Some keepers stay in the center and react to the shot. Doing this gives them a better chance in less perfectly placed balls.

- Some keepers guess which way the kicker is going and take a dive in that direction when the ball is touched. Doing so might result in a save, but keepers can look absurd if they guess wrong.

- A keeper can stretch out an arm in one direction or set up slightly off center. Doing this frequently deters the shooter from going that way. Then the keeper can dive in the other direction.

Shooter Strategies

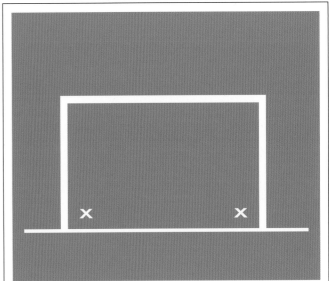

- The shooter needs to hit the goal. Even if the keeper gets a hand on the ball, there's a chance for a second shot. There's no chance for missed goals.

- The shooter should aim for the two lower corners.

- The kick doesn't need to be powerful as much as it needs to be accurate. A low roller to the corner will be impossible for nearly every goalkeeper out there.

- A kicker needs to know where the shot is going before he takes his first step toward the ball.

4-4-2 FLAT

Follow current philosophy and adopt the most popular formation of today

The 4-4-2 formation began in Great Britain and quickly spread throughout the world of soccer. It is without a doubt the most common formation in soccer today, although coaches are constantly fiddling with it to find the next greatest winning formation.

In the 4-4-2 formation, a coach puts in four defenders, four midfielders, and two forwards. The advantage to this formation over the 4-3-3 is that it beefs up the midfield strength. Midfield is important because it's where the transition game begins, taking the ball from the defensive end onto attack. Too many times the defense clears the ball, and then an ineffective midfield allows it to be sent right back.

Attack

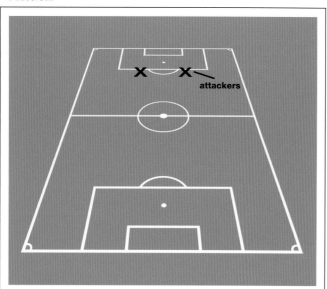

Midfield

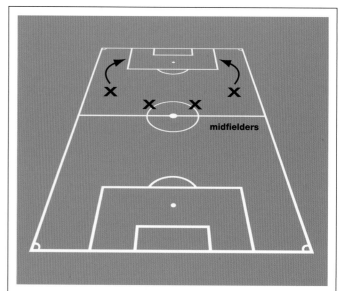

- The two forwards on the attack are both considered the center forward. They should not feel constrained to a left side or a right side.

- The forwards switch back and forth right and left and forward and back. Anything they do should be done in an effort to confuse the defense and open up space.

- The two outside midfielders should always be moving up the sideline on attack, forcing the defense to spread out and open up spaces.

- The other two midfielders both support and attack.

- This formation depends on a strong midfield. The midfield wing players are part of both the attack and the defense.

- Coaches should look for players who are fit, fast, and smart in order to fill all these wing positions.

- The two center players are fairly flat, holding the middle, but obviously they can shift forward and back, depending on the need.

Also, in a defensive game the midfield can hang back. Because defense is so important, the 4-4-2 allows the possibility of overloading the defense. When the other team is on attack, this defense allows for eight players to be marking up and defending the goal. Almost no team will have eight attackers, so this is a tremendous defensive advantage. On the flip side, if your team appears to be dominating, the four midfielders can push up and be mainly on attack. Coaches need to spend time training their midfielders to work this system on attack, or else the formation will prove very weak on the offensive side.

ZOOM

This formation is so popular today that there's a magazine in Great Britain entitled *FourFourTwo*. The magazine also has a website, www.four fourtwo.com, where it discusses the latest in soccer news.

Defense

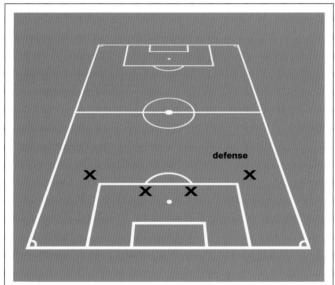

defense

- In this formation the defense moves as a unit, just as it did in the flat defense of the 4-3-3.

- Sometimes the flat defense can appear almost to be an arc, with the right and left defenders a little ahead of the center defenders.

- In a flat defense, there will be some opportunities for the wing defenders to spring out down the sideline for an overlapping attack.

- Coaches should look for speed when choosing their wing defenders in this formation.

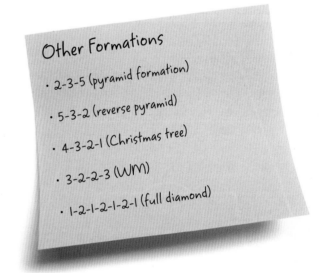

Other Formations

- 2-3-5 (pyramid formation)
- 5-3-2 (reverse pyramid)
- 4-3-2-1 (Christmas tree)
- 3-2-2-3 (WM)
- 1-2-1-2-1-2-1 (full diamond)

3-2-2 OR 2-3-2
Create a formation that works for younger players who play eight on a side

When you play with a full side of eleven players, you have a lot of tried-and-true formations to work with. College teams, World Cup teams, and professional soccer teams have done all the research and experimentation. You just have to pick the formation that you like best.

With the younger players—and therefore fewer players on

the field—it's a little trickier. (Most U-10 and younger teams play an eight-on-eight game, so that will be the focus in this book.) Not only do you have fewer players to work with, but also there's not a whole lot of professional research to rely on. Assuming you are playing eight on eight, you'll have one keeper and seven field players. Most coaches will use either a

KNACK COACHING YOUTH SOCCER

Using the 3-2-2

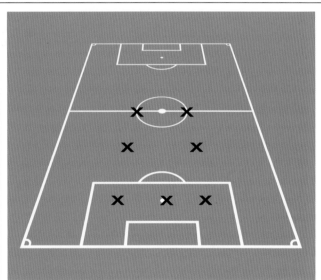

Using the 2-3-2

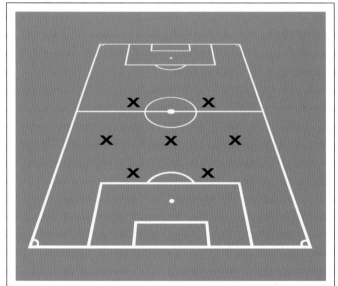

- If your team has a weakness, the last place you want it is on defense. The 3-2-2 works because you have three defenders usually going up against two forwards.

- Have your two wing players mark up man-to-man and let your center defender

pick up the slack.

- This formation puts a lot of stress on your midfielders because not only are they running goal to goal, but also they have to cover half of the field side to side. This situation could leave the center of the field vulnerable.

- The advantage to using the 2-3-2 is the heavy concentration in midfield. The team that controls the midfield controls the game.

- With three players across the field, there is less pressure for the outside mid-

fielders to cover the center of the field.

- Have your defenders play zone. Each defender gets half the field. They will have to shift and back up their fellow defender even if the ball is not on their side.

2-3-2 or a 3-2-2 formation in the game.

Not only do these formations provide a very balanced field, but also they allow the coach to be very specific with the players when teaching them about formations. A coach can tell a player, "You are the left defender" or "You are the attacker on the right," and the players will have a general sense of where they should be in relation to the other players on the field.

At this age the center of the field is critical. The players won't be strong enough or skilled enough to cross the ball in from the sideline. All your serious play will be centered in front of either goal. Because of this fact, you need to get your best players into the middle. If you want your best players to be more defensive, then go with the 3-2-2. That's the formation with the center defender. On the other hand, playing a 2-3-2 gives you more flexibility, with the center player able to switch from defense to offense as needed.

Positioning Thoughts

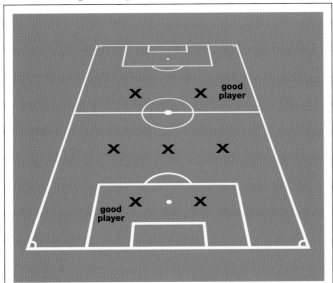

- At their age don't lock players into certain positions. Make sure you give everyone a chance to try different spots on the field.

- When there are two strong players on one team, many coaches will split them up. As an alternative, try putting them both on defense.

This will keep the ball out of the goal, and it may allow other players to blossom on attack.

- Don't put your best player in goal at this age. It's a waste of talent.

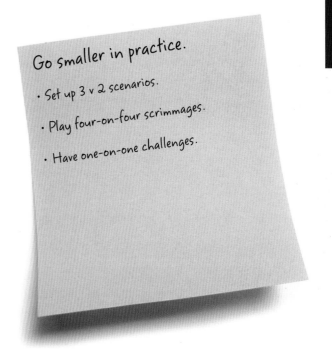

Go smaller in practice.

- Set up 3 v 2 scenarios.

- Play four-on-four scrimmages.

- Have one-on-one challenges.

2-1-2-2
Add a stopper, an alternative formation for an eight-on-eight game

As coach of a U-10 team, you'll find that your players mature and develop at vastly different rates. When they were four or five years old, there were a few standouts, but most of them were all swarming en masse and flailing at the ball at pretty much the same level. What a difference a few years can make.

By the time the players reach eight or ten, a few kids really do emerge from the pack. These players are usually natural athletes, and they usually have a fierce competitive streak. Every coach loves to have a player or two like them, but then a dilemma arises. Where to put these highly effective players? Do you make them strikers, so they can score goals? Do you put them at the last line of defense, just in case everyone else fails? Or do you use them as center midfielders so they can be everywhere at once? What's the best option?

Most coaches will agree that your strongest player should

The Stopper

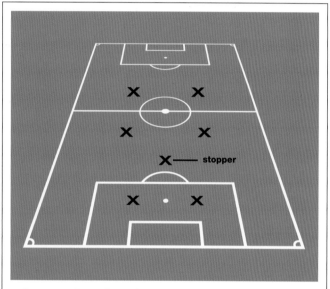

- Some coaches will argue that the stopper is the most valuable position on a soccer team.

- He controls the center of the field, he has a view of the entire attack in front of him, and he is the first line of defense.

- The stopper's goal is to keep the ball in the offensive end.

Advantages

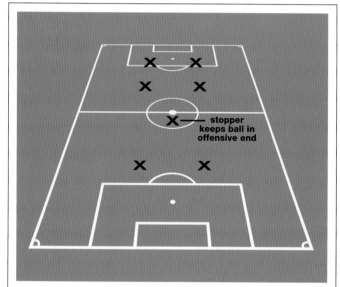

- If your stopper is a strong player, he'll keep the ball out of your defensive end of the field.

- Play will be concentrated in the middle of the field. This is where the action is going to happen in front of the goal. Players are not strong enough to really take advantage of spreading the field.

- Your defenders learn to stay tight in front of the goal instead of being spread out on the wings the way they would in a three-player defense.

be at the stopper position. The stopper is essentially placed between the midfielders and the defenders. As you know from an eleven-sided team, if you use a diamond formation, the stopper is the front of the diamond defense.

When you have only seven players, though, where's your stopper? Can you afford to have a whole "line of formation" for just one player? Many people feel strongly that the answer is yes. This is the basis for the 2-1-2-2 formation. The team will have two players at every standard position: two defenders, two midfielders, and two forwards. The stopper— the team's strongest player—should be placed between the midfield and the defenders.

Disadvantages of the 2-1-2-2

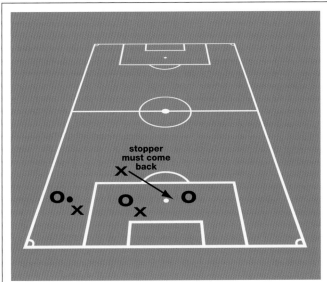

stopper must come back

Stopper Traits

• Is aggressive

• Is good at containing attack

• Is fast

• Can go man-to-man on best player

• You've overloaded your defense, so your attack will be weaker.

• You have no line with three across, so it's hard to use the sideline effectively

without completely tiring your players.

• Your players may have trouble learning to spread out and move to the open spaces.

SUPER SMALL
Basics of formation for the youngest players

With the youngest kids, there's not much point in teaching formations. They're all going to want to touch the ball, and more often than not, they're going to look like a swarm of bees as they move as one big group all around the field.

The number of players on a team in these leagues or camps or clinics is all over the map. However, the prevailing thought about play for this young age is that the fewer players on the field, the better because that means each child touches the ball more. A three-on-three game would be fine. Theorem 1 of youth soccer: The number of touches on the ball decreases as number of players increases. Clinics and camps will probably stick with the very smallest numbers: three on three and four on four. In this case, you don't want to mention a word about positions or formations.

If you're coaching this age, however, it probably means that you have a team that's in a league, not a group in a clinic. In

Set-up

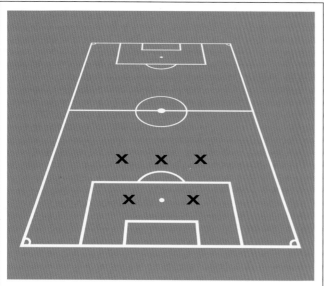

- If you have a five-on-five game, try a 3-2 or a 2-3. If it's six-on-six game, go for three each.

- Talk about how some players are there to protect the goal. These are the defenders.

- Others are there to attack the opponent's goal. These are the attackers.

- At their age, you don't want to introduce the concept of midfielders. Essentially all the players are midfielders anyway.

Don't Rock the Boat

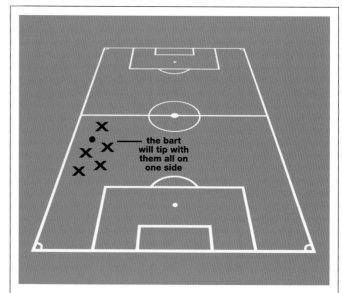

the bart will tip with them all on one side

- A fun way to teach the basics of staying spread out is to talk about the scrimmage as a pirate ship.

- Before the kids play, tell them how the ship will tip over if they're all on one side. They need to spread out in order to balance the ship.

- Then, as they're playing, yell out that the ship is sinking. Players need to spread out.

this case, the league will probably do something more like a five on five or a six on six. If you do have this many players, you can start to teach the basics of formation.

The Goalkeeper

Why Play Small?

- Offers better coach-to-player ratio

- Allows more touches on the ball

- Has more soccer decisions

- Lets the game teach the players

- At this age, many leagues do not have goalkeepers. Kids love to score, so the more opportunities, the better.

- For goals many leagues usually use cones that are placed roughly 4 feet apart, which makes scoring plenty tricky anyway.

- If your league does use keepers, then it's a good idea to just rotate everyone through the position. Don't pigeonhole players at this young age, and they usually all want to have a shot at it anyway.

INDIVIDUAL SKILLS
Teach your players how to contain, control, and confront the dribbling attacker

Defensive strategy changes with the ages of players. When your kids are very young, tell your defenders that their job is to stay back in front of the goal. However, as they age, you want to push that defense forward, so that you create a defensive wall far away from your goal. If you can keep the ball in the opponent's end of the field, you're much more likely to score and not be scored upon.

When the ball sneaks past your defense, and everyone has to scramble to get back and protect the goal, it's important for a defender to have the individual defensive skills to know how to slow the attack.

A coach always has a number of players, not just one, on

The Three C's of Defense

• Containment

• Control

• Confrontation

Containment

- The defender should go out to meet the dribbler without getting so close that the dribbler can make a move around him.

- In this situation, the defender who is guarding the player with the ball must do his best to slow the

- player. This action is called "containing" the player.

- The defender should not try to go for the ball.

- Containing a player allows the rest of the defense to get back into place.

defense, so no matter what the situation, one player will be on the ball, and the rest will be backups. If the transition has been quick, and your defense is scrambling to get back into position, then the defender who meets the ball has a responsibility to slow that player. He shouldn't make any bold moves that might result in a fake-out, but he should get in the player's way, which will slow the dribbler and maybe force a mistake.

Even if there isn't a breakaway situation, a defender might want to use this strategy anyway. As an attacker approaches, a defender has to decide what to do.

If the dribbler is poor, there might be an opportunity to steal the ball. Usually, however, there isn't, but a defender can't just let the dribbler get off easy. He slows the ball first and patiently waits for the mistake.

No matter what, your defenders have to play tough. They need to be willing to use their bodies to fight for the ball and keep attackers from moving into the middle.

Control

- After a player has been contained, it's time to force him over to the side and away from the goal.

- A defender should be able to do a good job controlling where the attacker goes. By placing himself between the goal and the player, he can push the player out to the sideline and farther away from the goal.

- As long as the defender stays slightly off the dribbler and doesn't make a bold play for the ball, the dribbler should not be able to get around him.

Confrontation

- The defender should always be on the lookout for a mistake by the dribbler. The instant the ball gets too far out in front, the defender should make more of an attacking move to get the ball away.

- A defender can't risk a confrontation, however, if he doesn't have other defenders behind him.

- After he senses a mistake, he must move in quickly and aggressively. Any hesitation can mean the loss of the opportunity.

DEFENSIVE STRATEGY
Choose the defense that best suits your team

Players are important in defense, but those players also have to work together as a group in order to have an effective defense, with the defenders on the weak side (the side that doesn't have the ball) backing up the defenders on the ball side in case an attacker gets by.

You have to look at your team and decide which type of defensive strategy to use. Man-to-man defense is probably the easiest to teach, but if your team isn't fast, then such a

defense could be a disaster even if the players know exactly what they're supposed to do.

Zone defense protects against the really fast attacker, but it might leave a player unguarded at a crucial moment, especially likely with young and inexperienced defenders.

Some teams like a mix of both defenses. Frequently teams will use a sweeper, whose main job is to "clean up" the messes that get through the other defenders. The sweeper is not re-

Man-to-man

- Players each match up with a player from the opposing team.

- Defenders usually match up with attackers and midfielders with midfielders. If the numbers don't match exactly, unassigned players need to pick up unmarked opponents.

- Tell your players that their goal is to stay with their opponent and prevent him from touching the ball. This directive usually makes the job very clear to young players.

Zone

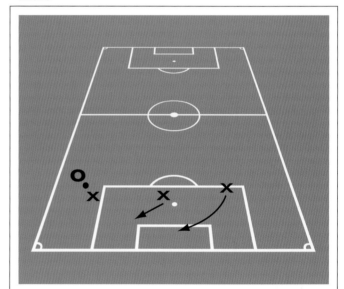

- Some coaches prefer a zone defense, although it is a little more difficult to explain than the man-to-man defense.

- If you have three defenders across the field, you can tell them that if the ball goes to one side, the player on that side goes out to meet the ball, the middle player shifts over and drops behind, and the far player shifts over and drops even farther behind.

- You can do the shifting in practice in slow motion, so the players get the idea.

sponsible for a specific person but rather is the backup for everyone. The downside, of course, is that you might have an attacker who is not marked up. When you play with a sweeper, you have to make sure that your midfield players know that they're responsible for marking up as well.

No matter which defense you choose, you need to impress upon your team the importance of communication. The keeper and sweeper should be especially vocal because those two positions are able to see the entire field before them. They should alert the defenders to an unmarked play-

er. If the sweeper needs to leave the middle of the field to help out, the keeper must call another defender back into the middle. The constant talking, shifting, and helping will make your defense strong.

Box and One

- Sometimes an opposing team has one real threat, and the rest of the team is mediocre. In that case, you want to try a zone defense in general, but one of your defenders will stay on the threat player.

- Choose a defender who's both fast and fit because you need him to stick with that player every moment.

- You also want someone who is good at individual defensive skills such as containing and controlling.

Defender Qualities

- Toughness

- Speed

- Sense of timing

- Big foot

THE WALL

Create an effective barrier to prevent the direct shot on goal

If the opponent gets a direct kick just outside the penalty box, many teams set up a defensive wall to get in the way of the shot. At lower levels of youth soccer, the wall is rarely necessary, but after the players develop strong kicks, then forming a wall against a direct kick is a strategy that most teams—even at the professional levels—employ.

When choosing who to put in your wall, you should look for specific qualities in your players. You want players who are tall and bold. You don't want players who will turn their backs to the ball. Technically, a wall should be 10 yards away from the kick, but many teams will move the wall in closer to force the player to ask the referee to move the wall back. If the kicker neglects to have the wall moved, then you've created quite an advantage because a closer wall blocks more area. If, on the other hand, the kicker does ask for the wall to be moved—which happens most of the time—then you've

Protection

- Many players are nervous about standing in the wall because they think it's going to hurt if the ball is kicked directly at them. They're right.

- In general, however, the wall acts as a deterrent, and the kicker usually avoids kicking directly at it.

- Players are allowed to protect especially sensitive parts of the body. Boys keep their hands down in front. Girls cross their arms across their chests.

Wall Strategies

- A team may have as few or as many players in the wall as it chooses. It may choose even to have no wall.

- A bigger wall covers more space, but it leaves the man-to-man coverage vulnerable.

- The closer your team is to the goal, the more people you want in your wall.

148

now given your defense a chance to set up before the kick. In general, this is a good strategy.

There is, however, one scenario you need to look out for. If a kicker gets the referee involved, then the kicker may not kick until the referee blows his whistle. But if a kicker doesn't ask for referee interference, he is free to kick the ball at any time. Some teams use this fast direct kick to catch opponents off guard when the opponents are busy setting up their wall. Make sure your players understand the rules of the game.

DEFENSE

Keeper Directs

- The keeper should take charge of the wall. She should tell the players how many players she wants in the wall and where she wants them to stand. she usually wants to line them up on the near post.

- One player should be the anchor. The keeper will stand on the near post and direct the anchor left or right.

- Everyone else should line up shoulder to shoulder with that anchor. There shouldn't be any gaps.

Placement

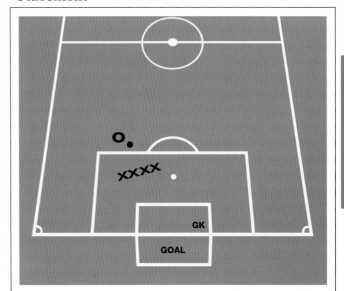

- The point of the wall is to block the near area of the goal, while the goalkeeper takes the far area.

- The edge of the wall needs to fully cover the near post area of the goal. If your team leaves that open, your team is completely vulnerable because the keeper will be all the way on the other side.

- Unless the other team has a huge kicker, you don't need to bother setting up a wall if the ball is more than 30 yards out.

EXTRAS
Tips for taking your defense to a new level of competency

In addition to the standard strategies, there are lots of ways by which you can both maximize and personalize your defense to fit your team. You also might change your defense if the opponents are offering a different challenge than you're used to. It might be a star player whom you need to shut down, or the other team might be leaps and bounds ahead of yours in speed or skill.

Perhaps you need to overload your defense to keep your team in the game. Over the past few decades professional soccer has switched from an offense-oriented game to a defense-oriented game. The most popular formation in the sixties and the seventies had only two defenders and three midfielders, yet it had five attackers. Now the most popular formation has four defenders, four midfielders, and two attackers.

However, don't take this reasoning to an extreme. So often when a team has a lead, it thinks it should move everyone

Double Team

- One strategy for marking a strong player is to double team the player whenever he or she has the ball.

- Another use of the double team is to gain an advantage, regardless of who has the ball. If one player is do-

- ing a good job containing an attacker, another player can come in to double team and perhaps steal the ball.

- The downside of double teaming is that it leaves an unmarked player.

Pushing Up

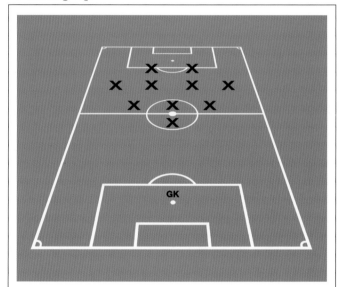

- Most teams like their defense to push up to the midfield when they are on offense. This way, they can be there to pop the ball back in if it starts heading into their end.

- Because of the offsides rule, pushing up keeps the offense out of your end.

- If your team's defense is being beaten regularly, however, then adjust your strategy.

- If you don't push up, you protect your goal more, but you end up ceding the middle of the field.

back on defense in order to preserve it. Doing this is a mistake. If you don't have some offensive players, you're going to have no one to distribute the ball to when you're trying to clear it out of your defensive area. The ball ends up coming right back in, and it never allows your defensive unit or keeper to get a rest. It actually makes the situation more dangerous than if you just left your team as it was. The best defense is a good offense.

Here are some more strategies that you may want to employ when you teach your team defense.

The Box

- Any foul committed by the defense that happens inside the penalty box results in a penalty kick. Players need to be aware of where the box starts.

- Defensively, they need to be really careful about committing a foul.

- Offensively, they need to be superaggressive to perhaps draw a foul.

Slide Tackle

In some leagues this is against the rules and will draw a yellow or red card.

- Slide tackles are almost exclusively used by defenders.

- Slide tackling is not always favored by coaches because it frequently results in a foul rather than a successful tackle. It also leaves the tackler on the ground.

- When a player slide tackles an opponent, he must be going for the ball only. If he ends up contacting the opponent in any way or tackling from behind, it means a direct kick for the other team.

- A successful tackle can stop a breakaway.

SET PLAYS
Train your players to defend against the opponent's set plays

All set plays take a lot of training time. If you're going to use set plays in a game, then you're going to have to make a significant commitment to practicing them. Some of them, such as the offsides trap, could actually be dangerous if your players aren't well tuned to the play.

Quite a bit of coaching in youth soccer depends on the abilities of your team and those of opponents. If you're coaching at the youngest levels, you certainly won't ever have to deal

with an opponent who has a set play, and you won't want to run one yourself. Even at the middle levels it's unlikely that you'll have opponents who have a set play. Even if they get the concept, their skill level may not allow them to execute the play well. But as you move up with your players as they age, the skill levels will increase, and the team that comes up with an effective set play will be at a distinct advantage if your team hasn't prepared for that possibility.

Offsides Trap

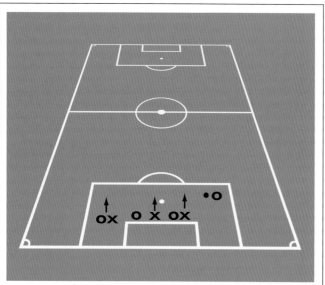

- Because the offsides rule requires a player to have two defenders (one is usually the keeper) between him and the goal, you can teach your players to create an offsides situation.

- The easiest time to implement this situation when first starting would be

  when your team is defending a direct kick.

- Right before the kick is taken, your entire defense takes two steps forward, leaving the offensive players offsides. Don't wait until the kick has been taken, however, because then the players would not be offsides.

Offense on Wall

- One strategy on a direct kick is to place an offensive player either in the middle of the wall or in front of the wall.

- The goal of this strategy is to distract the players in the wall as well as the keeper.

- Tell your defenders in the wall to stay tight and do their job as a wall. The other defenders will mark up the players.

Set plays or not, you also need to adjust your defense based on advancing skills. Take throw-ins, for example. At the younger levels, players can get throw-ins roughly 10 yards at the most. You'll defend that throw-in differently than you would a throw-in that goes almost all the way into the penalty box.

There's nothing worse than a ball thrown over your defender's head.

Drop Ball

- Figure out which of your players have the fastest reflexes. They'll be your drop ball kickers.

- If your team is in its defensive zone, you have to set up assuming that your player will not win the kick.

- Place two defenders in a triangle formation with the kicker. Doing this will help your team get to the ball first should the opponent win the kick.

Throw-in

- If the opposing team is in your team's defensive end, you'll want your players to mark up tightly.

- They may think they need to stand in front of the opponents to prevent them from getting the ball, but you need to instruct them to stay on the goal side of their players.

- If the opponents are in their end, then you want to mark the line tightly in order to tempt them to throw the ball into the middle of the field.

DRILLS
Good drills teach defensive skills and strategies

Defensive know-how is a tricky thing to teach. You need to spend time in practice covering both individual defensive skills and the big-picture team defensive skills. The tough part is that no matter how many drills you run in practice, it's never quite the same as playing in a game. Many players who demonstrate perfect knowledge of the three C's of defense will find that their skills disappear when they try to execute them at game speed.

So, that said, be sure to include scrimmaging in every practice. If you have a practice that's focusing on defense, then start your scrimmage a little early. In general, you don't want to interrupt your scrimmages too much, but if you leave a good amount of time at the end for that uninterrupted scrimmage, you can use the early part to focus on defense.

Blow the whistle and have the players freeze. Doing this will expose the players who are not sticking with their man-to-

5 versus 3

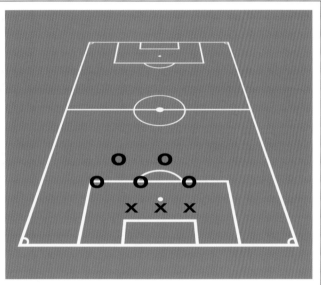

- Setting up a game situation in front of the goal is probably the best way to teach defense positioning and strategy.

- You want to make it extra challenging for the defense by having it be outnumbered. Using five offensive players against three

- defensive players usually works well.

- Show the players how one of them needs to go out and challenge the ball while the others do their best to back up and cover the other players.

Monkey in the Middle

- Although Monkey in the Middle can be played with any number of players, it's a great defensive tool to play a five-on-two game.

- The two defenders learn how to work together. One should call "ball" and move up to challenge the player with the ball.

- The other defender is the backup and tries to anticipate the passing and reduce the choices that the passer has. He should stay more in the middle to defend several possibilities.

man assignment. It will also help to educate players in how to shift and back up if your team is playing zone defense.

This is also a good time to remind your team of the importance of communication. A defender who is beaten by his player should immediately call for help. Another easy communication tactic for defenders is to yell "Switch!" when players are moving around in the box.

If the defensive team has fewer players than the players on offense, the sweeper should call back a forward to mark a player as needed. The defenders should always want to mark the players who are the biggest threat (closest to the goal) first.

One on One

- Divide players into pairs, with one ball for each pair.

- One member of each pair should try to dribble from one line to the next. The other player is the defender.

- First the defender should try to contain the dribbler.

He shouldn't go for the ball at all but rather make sure that the dribbler makes the slowest progress possible.

- On the next run-through, the defender should try to steal the ball.

Defending a Cone

- Another great way to work on defense is to have two players defending a cone.

- Divide your players into groups of roughly four passers and two defenders each.

- The passers try to knock over the cone from any direction, while the defenders try to not only protect the cone but also steal the ball.

GETTING DOWN THE FIELD
Teach your team to tackle, pass, and score

When you think about offense and defense in soccer, you should think more about basketball than a sport such as football. Although there are mostly defensive players and mostly offensive players, it's essentially a whole-team transition, the way it is in basketball. The instant your team gets the ball, all players should consider themselves offensive players.

Now it's time for them to pass the ball down the field and score. But passing is easier said than done. If the other team's defensive players do their job, they'll mark up on your players, and your players won't have too many passing opportunities. Instead you need to create the opportunities. Tactics such as overlaps, give-and-go plays, switching fields, and through balls are efforts to get a player open to receive a ball.

In the overlap, a player in a back line makes a run along the outside, up past the players in the line in front. Hopefully, the defenders will not be prepared for it.

Overlap

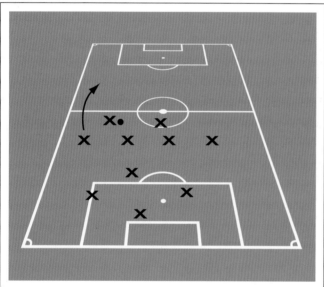

- The most effective use of the overlap is when the forward comes back for the ball.

- At this point the midfielder should sprint forward to take the attacker's position.

- Another opportunity can arise when a defender overlaps a midfielder in transition.

- To be their most effective, overlaps should be done near the sideline.

Give and Go

- When a player is confronted by a defender, passing the ball to an open teammate is the safest way to go.

- If this player then sprints by the defender, he can receive the ball back again. This play is called a "give and go."

- Give-and-go passes are typically short, quick passes.

Similarly, when your team switches fields, you hope to catch the other team unaware. If play has been dominant on one side of the field, it's natural for everyone to drift closer and closer to the play. A quick shift to a player on the opposite side will frequently result in progress down the field.

Give-and-go plays and plays in which the ball is either chipped over or played through the defense are a different story and take some skill and anticipation on the part of your players. Have them practice these plays, so they'll learn to ex-pect them. A perfect chip to an open space won't do your team much good if no one is running on to it.

Players should be constantly communicating these changes to their teammates.

Switching Positions

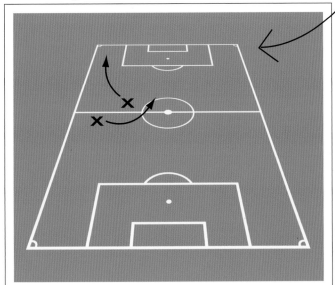

- Sometimes a player who usually plays in the center will find himself pulled over to the sideline.

- When this happens, the wing player should take over the center position.

- Player should always be thinking about filling the holes on the field. These's no point in having two players in the same spot.

Open Space

- The offensive strategy of playing a ball to an open space and having your team run onto it is smart if you have a quick team.

- The ball should be played in an area where the keeper cannot come out to save it.

- It is then the job of your attackers to get to the ball first to create a scoring opportunity.

- If you use this play too often, however, a team will just move its defenders back, and the play will no longer be effective.

THROW-IN STRATEGY
Teach more than just technique when it comes to throw-ins

Many coaches work on the mechanics of a throw-in but don't bother with any other aspect. Doing this is a mistake. The throw-in is a possession for your team, and you need to teach your players first to take advantage of the opportunities it allows and second how to maintain possession even if your team can't turn the thrown-in into an offensive threat.

When the ball goes out of bounds, the referee will blow his whistle to signal that the play has stopped and must be restarted with a throw-in. He will point in the direction of the throw, but he won't blow his whistle again. A player can throw in the ball immediately. Frequently a quick throw can give a team a huge advantage, especially at the younger levels when players are not used to players capitalizing on this part of the rules. The defense doesn't have time to mark up or move into proper defensive position. Teach your players to pick up the ball and throw it in quickly. Also teach them to

Which End?

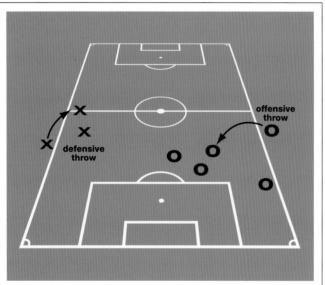

- When your team is down in its defensive end of the field, you want your team to throw the ball down the line, keeping it away from your opponent's best scoring opportunities.

- Because your defender will most likely be taking the throw, you want to make sure that your sweeper slides over in case of a turnover.

- In the offensive end of the field, either down the line or into the middle is an acceptable place to throw.

Long Ball

- A long ball is a throw that goes high over everyone's head.

- The long ball can be extremely effective when you have a quick team that can usually outrun the opponents when chasing a loose ball.

- For this throw to be the most effective, you want the throw-in to be very quick.

- If you have one player who can throw a really long ball, have him take most of the throws.

expect the quick throw from their teammates.

Usually you want your defenders taking the throw-ins. Push your midfielders and your forwards up to receive the ball. If your team is down in front of the opponent's goal, then your midfielders will probably take the throw because you don't want to pull your defenders too far out of position. Of course, if you have a player who can throw considerably farther than other players, you may want to consider having him take all the throw-ins.

Short Ball

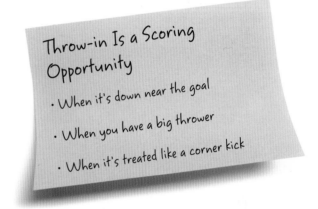

Throw-in Is a Scoring Opportunity
- When it's down near the goal
- When you have a big thrower
- When it's treated like a corner kick

- Many players will just throw the ball without thinking about what would be best for their teammate. This tactic might work for a long throw, but if a thrower is trying to reach someone close, there are better options.

- The thrower wants to throw the ball in a downward direction so that it lands at the teammate's feet.

- He also does not want to throw the ball so hard that it bounces off his teammate.

OFFENSE/TRANSITIONS

OFFENSE DRILLS
Teach players big-picture offense with small-sided drills

When you're trying to teach offensive and transition strategy through minidrills, the big picture frequently gets lost. The players don't have a sense of what you're trying to teach them. Because of that fact, many coaches try to set up gamelike scenarios without the other distractions of actually playing a full game. Every coach should employ this excellent teaching tool.

You might set up a five-on-three situation or a four-on-six situation. These create the aura of a gamelike situation but al-low you the opportunity to stop the play, reposition players, or redirect the pass. If you run them repeatedly, then eventually the concepts will sink in.

The main downside to this teaching tool is that it can get pretty boring. But if you put it in the middle, between some fun games, you'll achieve your teaching goals and still create an aura of fun for the players.

The other problem is that this tool doesn't involve the whole

Four-cones Drill

- Divide the team into groups of four. For each group, set up four cones—about 15 feet apart—in a square.

- Three players stand by one cone each. The fourth player is the defender and is in the middle of the square.

- One player passes the ball to another. The third player should run to the cone that will give the receiver two options for passing. In other words, he should never be diagonally across from the player with the ball.

2 versus 1

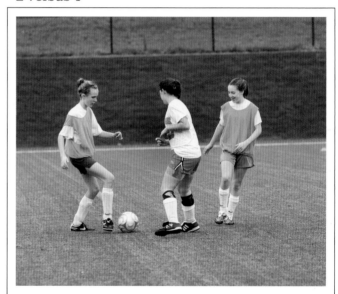

- Divide your players into three lines. One line is the defender line and should come in from the sideline. The other two are at-tack, and they come from midfield.

- Have the defender confront the player with the ball. That player should then pass the ball to his team-mate (the player in the other attack line) and then sprint forward to receive a pass back.

- The second player should pass the ball back, assum-ing that the defense follows the ball.

team. If you have two coaches, then you'll be able to divide your players into two groups, each working at its own end of the field. If you're going it alone, then you'll have to find a way to keep the extra players busy while you work with the others. One good way is to set up a Monkey in the Middle game outside the playing area but nearby. If you have more players, set up two games. Make sure the numbers match the numbers that you're working with on the field. Rotate the groups through the field, so that each spends a chunk of time with you.

········· YELLOW ● LIGHT ·········

Although setting up situations can be a helpful coaching tool, it can get really boring. Try to sandwich situations in between drills that are games, which are a lot more fun, and the scrimmage, which is also fun and will help reinforce the positioning you just worked on.

6 versus 3

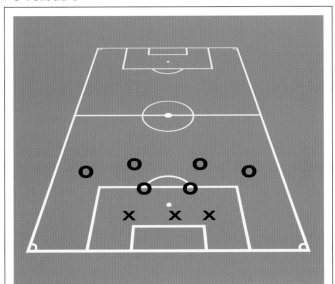

- Set up three defenders in front of the goal. Now set up six attackers in some semblance of the formation you'll use in a game. For example, if you use three midfielders and three forwards, set up that way.

- Have the attackers bring the ball from midfield and try to score. You may want to require that they pass three times before they can shoot.

- Because of the large imbalance in numbers, they should be successful most of the time.

3 versus 2

- Choose two players to be defense and one to be goalkeeper. The rest of the players go to midfield and line up in three lines, spread out across the field.

- The first three players bring the ball down and try to score. If they score, they take the place of the keeper and defenders. If they are stopped, they return to the lines.

- The object is to try to stay on defense as long as possible.

OFFENSE/TRANSITIONS

TRANSITIONING

The philosophy behind transitioning is that offense begins with defense

Usually the offense begins with a tackle by a defender. That is the moment of transition and should be taken seriously. Too often a defender will just boot the ball as far as possible. Although doing so might have the short-term benefit of getting the ball away from the goal, it doesn't set up an effective plan to keep the ball in your team's possession. A big

boot one way usually ends up with another boot right back at your team. And a soccer game that looks like pinball isn't a good thing.

Ideally, your transition should begin with an outlet pass. As soon as a defender makes a tackle, the wing players, either defenders or midfielders, should spring to the sidelines,

One on One

- Usually transition begins with a tackle.

- When a defender successfully takes the ball away, he should look for an outlet pass and push forward.

- Then the team must change into an offensive formation, providing support players to continue moving up the field.

Maintaining Formation

- Transition requires effort by the entire team.

- If the offense pushes forward without the support of the midfield and defense, the ball will just come right back.

- Each time the ball is moved up the field, all players should move as one unit to keep the passing triangles in place.

- It is the job of the sweeper to push the team forward.

awaiting a pass. The sidelines are usually wide open because players tend to drift into the middle where the goal is. That's the last place your team wants the ball. So, aside from getting the ball away from the goal, this outlet pass will allow your team to keep possession, keep the ball away from the opponents, and give the team a few precious seconds to make the mental and physical transition to offense.

But transition isn't about just defenders and midfielders. Teams that are successful in a quick transition are those teams whose forwards are willing to come back for the ball.

A forward who just stands and waits for the ball to get to him will still be waiting at the end of the game. He shouldn't get in the way, but he should come back and put himself into a position to receive a pass.

Defense as Offense

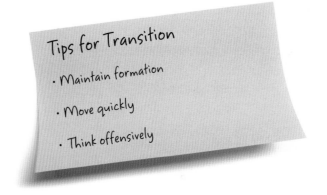

Tips for Transition

• Maintain formation

• Move quickly

• Think offensively

- As soon as their team has the ball, defenders should consider themselves part of the offense.

- Many times your defenders are the players with the strongest kicks, and therefore they can score a goal from far out.

- Overlapping the midfielders will also occasionally put your defenders into scoring position.

TRANSITION DRILLS
Big-picture scrimmage drills help with transition

Teaching transition to your players is extremely difficult, especially at the youngest age levels. Don't even think of teaching transition until the players have reached the ages of eleven to fourteen, and even then don't get discouraged if the concept escapes them. Frankly, they're probably using a lot of transition concepts without even realizing it.

However, your players can do a number of drills that will help them learn how to switch their mind-set from offense to defense quickly. These drills will help the players to learn the concept without even knowing it. Most of these drills need at least a half-field and sometimes a full field. They tend to be less fun than some of the games, so throw one or two of these drills into practice but then move on. If you repeat them often enough over the course of the season, then the transition concept will begin to sink in.

You can get the concept across to the younger kids by hav-

Miniside Goals

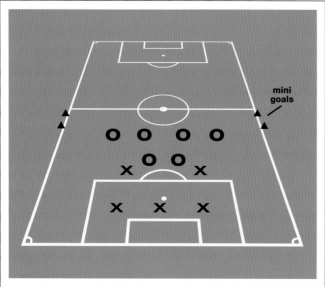

mini goals

- Play on half the field. Split your team into two teams: one offense, one defense.

- The offense wants to score on the regular goal. The defense will have two minigoals at midfield on the outside of the field.

- This situation forces the defense not only to clear the ball to the outside but also to begin transitioning into offense.

Outlet Pass Drill

- Play a five-versus-five game in front of a goal—no goal-keeper.

- The instant the defense gets the ball, a teammate should sprint to the sideline and call for the ball.

- To make this drill more competitive, if the defense completes this pass, it gets a point.

- The offense gets a point when it scores a goal.

ing them yell "Attack" after their team gains possession of the ball. Doing this helps cement the idea that the entire team, including the defenders, is on offense now. And because there are two teams, one team will be yelling with every change of possession. Most kids love to have permission to yell, so doing this is usually a big hit. The other fun thing about soccer is that the possession will switch back and forth constantly, so the kids will have numerous opportunities to grasp the idea that the whole team switches to offense.

Middle Box

- Mark off a 20-by-20-foot box in the center of the field between the 18 and the midfield. This is the dead zone for both teams.

- Now the teams have a miniscrimmage, trying to work around this dead zone.

- The defense learns to bring the ball to the outside.

- The offense learns to bring the ball down the wing.

3 versus 3 versus 3

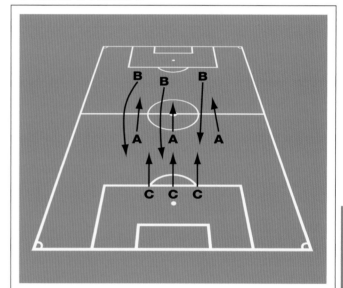

- This is a full-field drill. Divide your players into groups of three.

- A group of three starts in the midfield and dribbles toward another group of three, trying to score.

- If the group scores or the defensive group manages to steal the ball, it goes in the other direction against a third group of three.

- The original group lines up as defense against the third group, which will be coming down the field soon.

OFFENSE/TRANSITIONS

GAMES FOR 7- TO 10-YEAR-OLDS

Use games and competition to provide fun and learning at the same time

By the time your players are in the middle age range, they will get the concept that part of soccer practice is about learning and improving. But that doesn't mean that they're going to love doing just drills. Games are still a great way to keep them learning and keep them loving both the game of soccer and practice time.

But that doesn't mean you have to ignore the learning aspect of practice. When you begin a drill, always explain why the drill will help them become better soccer players. Not only will doing this help them perform better in the drill, but also they may actually focus more on the specific aspect that the drill has been designed for. When the drill is over, make

3 v 3

You can even keep track of who wins each of the games and have a winning team at the end.

- Creating a very small scrimmage of three on three is always a great drill. You can have several of these scrimmages going at once.

- Not only does doing this force all the kids to get involved in the game, but also they all have to work on offense, transition, and defense. There's no sticking to position.

- If you have several three-on-three games going at once, then you can rotate whom the teams play every five minutes or so to keep it interesting.

Leg Goals

- If your players divide nicely into groups of four, you can set up a one-on-one game in between two players who stand with their legs apart.

- Players have to get the ball through the opponent's leg goal in order to score.

- Have them play hard for three minutes and then switch. The players become the goals, and the goals become the players.

sure you ask the players to state how it helped them. Doing this forces them to think about the game in soccer terms.

Have them explain skills or drills to other members of the team. Or you can have them demonstrate a specific skill or concept. This is a classic teaching tool. In general, students remember a small percentage of what they read or hear, a much bigger percentage of what they see, and an even bigger percentage of what they do. However, the biggest retention of them all is what students teach.

2 versus 1 While 1 versus 1

- Divide your team into groups of five. Each group plays in two marked-off zones.

- Two pinnied players play Keep Away against a shirt player in one zone, while at the same time a shirt player tries to stay with a pinnied player who is making runs to get free in the other zone.

- After three passes, the pinnied players have to pass to their teammate.

- The player not involved in the pass runs over to the new zone and then begins playing Keep Away. And so on.

Scores on the Doors

- Divide the players into two teams. One team is the door team, and the other team is passers. The doors are two players holding a pinny between them.

- The passers have to try to pass the ball through the doors.

- The doors move around the field to try to avoid the ball pass through them.

173

TEAM GAMES

Once the players age a bit, the value of repetition goes away and now more variety means more fun

Before every practice you should sit down and plan your practice. You don't have to go crazy and have a minute-by-minute schedule, but you should have a general idea of what new skills or strategies you want to teach, what old skills need refining, and in general what your players need to work on.

After you have a general sense of what you want the practice to cover, you should then break it down into more specific drills and games. Balance the drills with the games, so that teaching and fun sort of blend together. Even if you don't use all the drills, or even if you get pressured to play again that favorite Steal the Bacon game that you deliberately left off the list, at least you'll have your ideas in front of you as a reminder.

Foosball

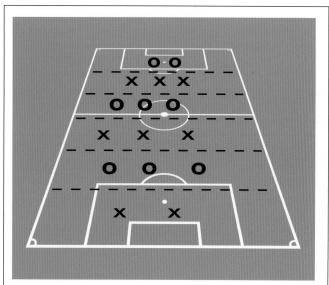

- Foosball is a table soccer game in which toy players are attached to rods across the table, with each team alternating every rod. You want to re-create this game on the field.

- Divide players into two teams and divide the field into four zones. Alternate teams within each zone.

- Now players must try to score, but they can't dribble out of their zone. They must pass the ball through the opponent's zone or boot it over the opponents in order to get it to their team-mates.

Feeder Ball

- Divide players into two teams, forming two lines at the top of the 18.

- Each team has a feeder with four balls outside the perimeter of the 18.

- Each team sends one player into the 18. A ball is sent in, and the two play until a goal is scored or the ball goes out of bounds. They then must chase after the ball and return it to their feeder.

- A team loses when it no longer has its four balls.

When you start out, you might think that such planning is overkill. You have a bunch of ideas, and you just run through them without a list. But as the season goes on, things will slip a little. Frequently coaches fall back on the drills that kids seem to like or ask for. The kids will definitely make their preferences known, and after all, you do want to please them.

But if you find yourself leaning too much on old favorites, you need to do a little planning because inevitably coaches fall into ruts. Some drills are just more productive than others, and some drills keep popping up because they're just plain easier to run. Although this isn't the worst thing that can happen, it won't help your team develop or grow as much as if you really take the time to plan your practice.

Soccer Marbles

- Play this game in the center circle. Every player has a ball.

- In marbles the idea is to get your opponent's marbles out of the circle by bumping them with your marble.

Adapted for soccer, the aim is to use your ball to bump out other players' balls. Last player left is the winner.

- An adaptation would be to divide the players into two teams to play this game.

Hot Potato

- All players start with a ball and dribble around inside the center circle.

- You yell, "Switch," and players must leave their ball and find a new ball.

- You kick one of the balls out of the circle.

- The player who ends up not having a ball is out of the game.

GAMES FOR 11- TO 14-YEAR-OLDS
A variety of games to ensure that everybody is playing soccer and having fun at the same time

If you've been with your team a long time, you probably view practice as a time to improve on the players' skills. You see the players getting older, more competent, and more multidimensional, and you want to capitalize on their new skills and knowledge. But keep in mind that these players are still kids.

Games are still important for this age. Although many of these kids are on the soccer field because they want to be good at soccer, ultimately they should be there because they view it as a fun activity. Remember that until these kids reach professional levels, sports are recreation, not work. Your goal should be to teach at the same time that the kids are having fun.

KNACK COACHING YOUTH SOCCER

Four Goals

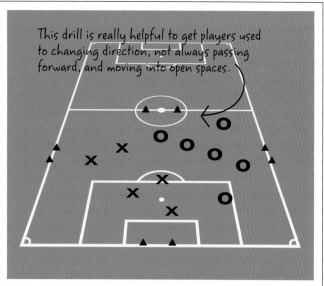

This drill is really helpful to get players used to changing direction, not always passing forward, and moving into open spaces.

- Divide your players into two teams. Using cones, set up four small goals, one on the end line, one on each sideline, and one on the midfield line.

- Each team is responsible for defending two of the goals.

- On defense, this game really helps players learn to mark up.

- On offense and transition, it helps players realize that there are more options than just kicking the ball forward.

Winning the Ball

- Divide the players into two teams. Both teams stand outside the 18, one team on each end of the box.

- Feed a ball into the center. The first two players sprint into the box and battle it out.

- The object is to control the ball long enough to pass it to their team. The ball must not go over the 18-yard line or the end line—only over the sides of the box.

- After everyone has gone, the team with the most successfully retrieved balls is the winner.

But the kids aren't the only ones who should be having fun. You need to make sure that coaching is a satisfying experience for you as well. Whether you're getting paid to coach or volunteering, you need to figure out how to make it a positive experience for you as well. Think about what you enjoy. Is it the teaching part you like, or is it really the soccer that brings you to the field? Or are you there entirely because you want to be part of your child's youth sports experience? How can you enhance the aspects of coaching that really bring you satisfaction? For instance, if you miss playing soccer and want to be out on the field, then jump into the scrimmage. The players usually love challenging the coach.

Through the Legs

- Divide your players into pairs. Each pair has one ball.

- One player should be on the end line and the other on the 6. The player on the 6 stands with legs apart and may not move.

- The player on the end line passes the ball through the legs of his partner. If he's successful, the partner does the same thing back.

- If ever a passer is unsuccessful, the pair is eliminated.

Scrimmage with Feeders

- Divide players into three teams of four. Play this game sideways on half a field. Two teams are on the field at once.

- The team that is off becomes the feeders, and each feeder should stand in one corner of the field.

- You call out a feeder's name. He passes the ball into the first open player to get into position. Teams try to score a goal on either goal.

- If a team scores, it remains on the field. The feeders become the new team, and the losing team becomes the feeders.

MORE GAMES: 11- TO 14-YEAR-OLDS
Tough coaches with tough practices aren't good in youth sports

Many former college and high school athletes end up coaching their children. For the most part, this situation is good. Such athletes are knowledgeable about their sport, and they usually have a passion for it as well. The tricky part comes when they try to treat youth sports as if they were high school or college sports. These children are supposed to be viewing the sport of soccer as a fun activity, not as a means to an end.

But former athletes are not the only coaches who fall into this trap. Sometimes you might have a parent who didn't get very far as an athlete when he was younger. He takes his coaching role models from movies. As wonderful as these movie coaches are, they're pretty unrealistic and frankly inappropriate as well.

So don't lose sight of your players' young age. Stay positive, keep it light, and have fun yourself. You also want to be sure

Pinnies and Shirts

For lower-level players, rotate the defenders every two or three minutes rather than automatically switching after loss of possession.

- Divide your players into three equal teams. Two teams play offense against one team whose members wear the pinnies.

- If the defense (the pinny team) is able to steal and clear the ball, the team of the player who made the mistake takes the pinnies and becomes defense.

- You can also just switch up individuals rather than a whole team.

Sharp Shooter

- One player starts in goal. The rest are in a line at the 18. You are a feeder.

- The first person shoots. If he misses the shot or the goalkeeper saves it, the shooter becomes the keeper, and the original goalkeeper goes to the shooting line.

- If the shooter makes it, on the other hand, he goes to the end of the line, and the next person in line loses his shooting spot and immediately becomes the keeper.

- The original goalkeeper is then eliminated.

to keep your comments positive. Children today are raised with positive feedback. They will be constantly seeking validation and praise from you because in general in today's society that's what they're getting at home. It wouldn't be unusual for a player to feel that the coach doesn't like him not because you've yelled, but merely because you haven't flattered him. And frankly, the more nice things you say about your players, the more positive you'll feel toward them. It works both ways.

Outlet Passing Game

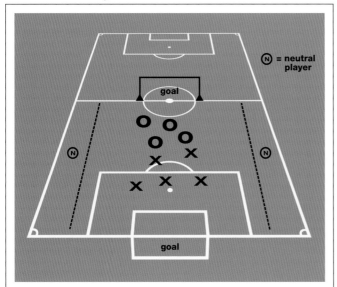

Three-team Scrimmage

- This game is played the regular way on half the field.

- You should mark off with disks a lane on the outside parts of the field, roughly extending the 18-yard line. These are the "safe" zones where a player can't be challenged. In each safe zone are two people who will be neutral players.

- A team needs to pass the ball into the safe zone before being able to go to goal.

- The safe zone player needs to pass the ball back to the same team he received the ball from.

- Divide your players into three teams. The game should be played sideways on half of the field to keep the field small.

- Two teams start the scrimmage. One team sits out.

- Teams play until a goal is scored. The team that scores the goal gets to stay on the field, and the other team goes off. The team that is sitting out comes in.

179

STRATEGY

Use field conditions, knowledge of your opponents, and your strengths

College teams have professional scouts who watch games and analyze opponents. They make videotapes and keep statistics, noting injuries, substitutions, and playing trends. They keep track of where the shots were taken or where the goalkeeper seemed vulnerable. Armed with all this helpful information, they report back to the coaches, and the coach-

es use this information when they plan their strategy for upcoming games.

In high school there might be a little scouting done, but it's mostly done by the coach himself—or maybe an assistant coach if there is one. In youth soccer official scouting would seem a bit excessive. But that doesn't mean that you should

Field Conditions

- A coach should walk the field before the game. If there are rocks or glass, he may want to remove them. If the field conditions are excessively bad, the referee should be notified.

- You should notice if the field is slanted in one direction. You should notice if

the goal mouth is worse on one end than the other.

- Finally, you should take a look at the sun. Is the sun going to be in a keeper's eyes? Is it going up or coming down? If it's going up, choose that side later. If it's coming down, take that side for the first half.

Player Strengths

- Although you shouldn't lock players into certain positions at a young age, you can play them more in one spot than another, depending on their skills.

- Know your players' strengths and weaknesses. Don't put a bunch of poor

dribblers together on offense. Mix some good ones in with bad ones.

- If you have a weak keeper in the goal, beef up your defense. If you have a few superstars on defense, then maybe you can afford to overload your offense.

ignore what you know about your opponents. Certainly if you've come up against a team before, you should use your knowledge of that team to plan your strategy. Maybe the team has one big scorer, and the rest of the team is weak. You might want to consider marking that player tightly or even double teaming her. It could be that that team has a striker who is incredibly fast. In that case, you might want to shuffle your players a bit so that your fastest player will be on defense marking the other team's fast player.

Tweaking your strategy is based on other factors as well.

What are the field conditions? Is one end sunny or muddy? Think about how you want to use that condition to your advantage.

Do you have any absences or injuries? If one of your key players is out of the lineup, how are you going to reshuffle the players? In order to get a strong lineup, you may have to switch a lot of players. Is doing that going to create too much confusion? Use your knowledge of your team to plan your best winning strategy.

Using Speed

- Speed is one of the most valuable traits a player can have.

- Many coaches think their team's speed needs to be on attack. Although this is true, you can't afford not to have speed on defense as well to counterbalance the opponent's attacking speed.

- Try to balance your speedy players throughout the field.

Playing Tough

- Value toughness over refined foot skills.

- The players who fight for every ball and are frequently on the ground are going to be strong players, regardless of their skills.

- A player who follows his shot, challenges the keeper, and drives to the goal will score more often than the player who has the pretty shot.

PREP

If you come prepared to the game, you'll have a much easier time coaching

Most young kids are not terribly focused. Little players are notorious for picking dandelions, doing cartwheels, or even wandering off the field. They really don't get the concept of staying focused on the game yet. If they're teenagers, they're out there chatting with their friends, talking about TV shows, the latest YouTube gross video, or who hooked up with whom. Either way, it's up to you to get them focused and ready to play.

To do that, you need to be focused and ready to play yourself. You can't be running back to your car to get your money for the referee or the players' cards. You can't be trying to pump up your deflated balls at the last minute. It's hard to prioritize volunteer coaching when you have a very busy life, but

Corner Flags

- The corner flags help the referee determine whether the ball went over the sideline or the end line.

- Many coaches are responsible for making sure that the corner flags are in place, especially if their game is the first game of the day.

- You need to factor in time to do this. If you have an early game, you need to arrive even earlier.

Balls at the Game

- Most coaches bring a bag of balls for pregame warm-up. If you don't have your own supply, you should ask each player to bring his or her own ball.

- In the ball bag, you should have a hand pump. Balls need to be reinflated with regularity.

- The home team generally provides the game ball. It should be the proper size, clean, and fully inflated.

spending a little extra time in advance will save you stress and headaches later. It will also show in your team's performance. A coach and players who are focused before the game are more likely to be focused during the game as well.

A focused and communicative coach will also win the hearts of the parents. Nothing is more frustrating as a parent than to have schedules or locations change or practices canceled or added on a whim. And if a coach is responsible about communicating with parents, then he is justified in demanding that parents communicate equally as responsibly.

Money

- The referees get paid in a variety of ways, but frequently it is the coaches who have to pay them.

- Be prepared. Be sure you have the cash on hand and that you know the correct amount.

- It might also be good to have extra money in case the ice cream truck drives by.

Cards

- In a traveling program, players must be registered with the state, and each will receive a player's card.

- Your soccer club will assist you with this process of getting your team carded.

- Every game you must bring these cards to show the referee. If a player does not have a card, he will not be able to play the game.

- Guard these cards with your life because if your players don't have their cards, you'll be forced to forfeit the game.

PLAY TIME

Deal with the subbing issue to keep all things equal or at least respectable

Dealing with the players' playing time is one of the hardest duties of a youth coach. Some leagues mandate playing time: equal time for all or at least half a game for a player. Other leagues are more like scholastic or professional sports; they're all about winning and have very few guidelines. Many are somewhere in between.

Most volunteer coaches of youth soccer end up in their positions purely by chance. They generally follow their own child into whatever league fits best. So, sometimes your coaching style and the league don't match. Needless to say, though, you're going to be the one who has to bend.

If you are in a situation where you do have to pay attention

Sheet of Paper

	Name:	#
1	Alyssa	11
2	AnnaMaria	23
3	Bryce	8
4	Caity	1
5	Dara	18
6	Eva	13
7	Jade	4
8	Karen	6
9	Kayla	44
10	Lauren	3
11	Minki	15
12	Nina K.	10
13	Nina P.	17
14	Samantha	2
15	Taylor	9
16	Vanessa	12

- Keeping track of the players is easier if you have a plan. If you have a lot of players, you may want to write out your subbing strategy ahead of time.

- Put in your strongest players right off the bat. Figure out who those players are.

- Or, knowing that you have to play everyone, you may want to put some weaker players in initially so that when you sub, the team's level of play doesn't drop dramatically.

- Writing it all out helps you figure out your team's strategy.

Positioning

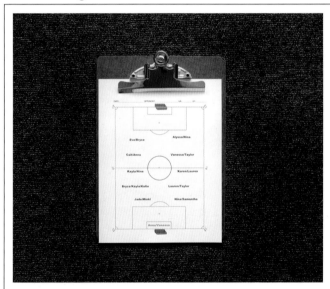

- Although you don't want to pigeonhole players into a certain position early in their career, plan it out as if you could. This is your ideal lineup.

- Now, when you put in your subs, try not to vary this lineup by more than one-third.

- When you switch your best attacker onto defense, make sure the rest of the defense is solid to cover any mistakes.

to subbing time, give it a little thought ahead of time. You have to figure out how you are going to best utilize all your players, not just your top eleven.

Although juggling the subs can be a pain, the liberal subbing rules in most youth leagues actually provides a coach with a tremendous opportunity for individual instruction. A coach can sub a player in order to give him a quick lesson. Then he can put the player right back in at the next opportunity.

In a similar vein, if a bench player is struggling with some aspect of the game, the coach can pull her up to the sideline and point out someone on the field who is doing that specific aspect correctly—even if that someone is on the other team. Now the player has a visual lesson of what she should be doing. The coach can then put her into the game to see if she can execute that problematic aspect.

Watch the Time

- When you have a large number of subs and an equal play time requirement, put the group in for timed shifts.

- For instance, if you have sixteen players, you'll have five sitting on the bench with ten field players and a keeper. In a thirty-minute half, put in the bench players after ten minutes. Then sub the remaining players on the field for the last ten minutes.

- This way, each player plays exactly two-thirds of the half.

- The downside is that you aren't subbing based on performance.

Resting Time

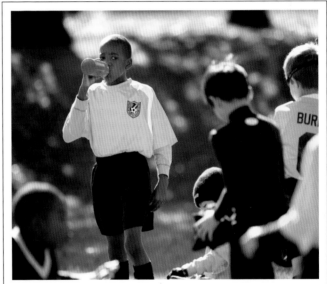

- If someone is getting beat to the ball on a regular basis, take him out and rest him, even if he is your most skilled player. You don't want your players conserving their energy on the field because they know you want to keep them in the whole game.

- Give them personal feedback when they come off the field and make sure you end on a positive note.

- On hot days you need to sub even more often in order to let your players drink water.

WARM-UP DRILLS

Use warm-up time for both the body and the mind

Warm-up time varies from team to team and coach to coach. As a coach, you communicate the game time. If you want players on the field forty-five minutes early, it's your prerogative. If you want to spend only fifteen minutes warming up, that's fine, too.

Field availability may play a role in your decision. If you're playing on a field that's wedged into a city block with not an iota of extra space, you might not want to get your players

there early only to sit and watch the game before theirs. If, however, your team has the first game of the day or if you know there's going to be plenty of time between games or lots of open space on the sideline, then you can choose the amount of time needed for warm-up.

Generally speaking, the older the players are and the more competitive the level of play, the longer the warm-up should be. Young players might need about fifteen minutes, where-

Keeper Warm-up

- If you have two keepers, have them toss the ball back and forth to each other while the rest of the players are doing their warm-up.

- Have them start on their knees and roll the ball to the sides so they can get

into the mind-set of rolling in the dirt and catching the ball on the ground.

- Then they should stand up and do some high tosses and jumps.

- Finally, they should shoot on each other for real.

Shuttle

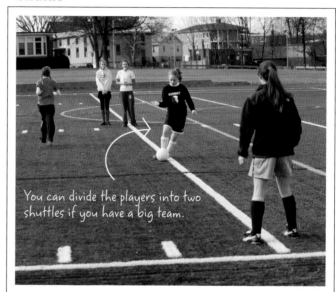

You can divide the players into two shuttles if you have a big team.

- Divide players into two lines, about 20 yards apart, facing each other. One line has the ball. The first person passes the ball to the other line, then runs to the end of the other line.

- The first person in the other line receives the ball and passes it back, again fol-

lowing her pass and going to the end of the opposite line.

- The shuttle is a good warm-up because it gets the players' blood pumping, and it gives them lots of touches on the ball without getting them too tired.

as U-14 teams might get to the field forty-five minutes before game time.

If you're coaching the littlest players, then warm-up time might be built in to your game time. Many leagues slot their four- and five-year-olds into an hour on the weekend, with a half-hour devoted to practice and a half-hour devoted to game time.

Stretching

- If your players are young, lead them in a few stretches after they've warmed up.

- If they're older, have the players stretch on their own. If you have captains, leading the stretches can be one of their responsibilities. Even if you change captains every game, those players should lead the stretches.

- You should allot five to ten minutes of your pregame time for stretching.

Shooting

- End the warm-up with a passing progression and a shot on goal. Doing this gets everyone in a game frame of mind.

- Make three lines at the midfield, balls in the middle line. Put in one defensive player and the keeper. The three front players in each line move toward the goal and take a shot.

- Rotate in a new defender and have the next three in line come down.

HALFTIME & WRAP-UP

Take time before, during, and after the game to get your players to focus on soccer

Soccer is unusual in the sports world in that it has no time-outs and very few opportunities to do any coaching from the sideline. You need to do most of your coaching in practice (which is a good thing, really). However, when the kids come off the field at halftime, this is your opportunity to get them thinking about one or two changes they may make when they go back out onto the field.

The first half of the game can also be used as a scouting opportunity. If you notice that one opposing player is dominating, then you can put one of your toughest defenders on him or double team him for the second half. Halftime is your chance to put your observations to good use.

Coach Talk

- Keep it simple, and keep it positive.

- Start off by talking about what the players are doing really well. Emphasize that you want to see them continue that in the second half.

- Now tell them about one or two things they need to improve upon.

- Finally, bring it full circle and be positive again before you send them out onto the field.

Hydrate

- Make sure all your players are drinking water during the halftime break.

- Many coaches ask parents to provide sports drinks or water for the team to ensure that everyone has a drink.

- Players can also benefit from orange slices or grapes.

The weather can affect your halftime strategy. When it's hot outside, you have to make sure your players don't chug too much water. And it might be worth losing part of your talking time to move them over to a shady spot and let them cool off.

When it's cold outside, you have to keep the players warm, especially goalkeepers. If they haven't been getting a ton of action, they are frequently cold when they come off the field. Sometimes their fingers are so cold that they're not moving well. It's a good idea to have hand warmers in another pair of gloves to warm them up during halftime.

GREEN ● LIGHT

Frequently parents are on the opposite side of the field from the coaches and players, but if they're not, you should always move your team out of earshot of the parents when you give your halftime and wrap-up talks. Doing this keeps the kids focused, and keeps parents from interfering with their own thoughts and strategies. This also has the advantage of taking you away from the opponents.

Player Feedback

- Give your players a minute or two of downtime for just general talk before you start your halftime spiel.

- A good way to get them to refocus on the game is to have them tell you what they've noticed on the field.

- Make sure they do not put their teammates down.

End-of-game Reminders

- Shake hands

- Warm down and stretch

- Give a wrap-up talk

- Clean up

PRACTICE FOR YOUNG PLAYERS
A sample practice uses the theme of ball control

The main goal for the littlest players is to keep them engaged and having fun, so your coaching should focus on getting them moving quickly rather than having them stand around and listen to instructions. Instructions can come later and little by little.

Aside from the many goofy or fun drills that are presented in this book, you can also try progression drills with this age group. Progression drills work well with all ages, but they are especially helpful with the youngest kids because you have to teach them only one piece of the drill at a time. Not only will you spend less time talking and more time playing, but also kids can really gain confidence by mastering a specific skill or drill. The more repetition you have, the closer they'll be to that ideal.

A progression drill is one that begins very simply, and then little by little more pieces are added to the same basic drill.

Pirate Warm-up

- Follow the drill on page 38.

- Greet the kids in a pirate voice. Remind them that they all need to say, "Aye, aye, Captain!" You'll set the stage immediately for a fun, silly practice.

- Spend five to ten minutes on this drill. Watch for signs of boredom. Make sure you ask the kids questions such as "Shall we make them walk the plank?" so they can say, "Aye, aye, Captain" a lot.

Ball Control Drills

- Use the idea of progression when you're teaching ball control.

- To start, players should throw the ball up into the air to themselves and see if they can get it under control quickly.

- Next have them pair up, one ball for each pair, and toss it back and forth to each other.

- Then have them drop the ball onto the ground and pass it back and forth with their feet. Make sure they get the ball under control before they send it back.

For instance, if you're teaching passing, have the kids pass the ball back and forth. After a few minutes, have them pass and move to a new spot. Then you can line them up and have them pass to each other while they move down the field. Finally, have them passing, moving down the field, and finally taking a shot on goal. Eventually you can throw a defender in there, too, if you want. That's a progression drill, although this particular example might be a little dull for the four- and five-year-olds.

MAKE IT EASY

If it's apparent that your players really enjoy one of the games that follows, have them play it in every practice. Don't play too long in one practice, but play it frequently. Kids love repetition, and usually they will enjoy a game more the tenth time they've played it than the first time they played it.

SAMPLE PRACTICES

Ball Control Games

- You can find ball control games in Chapter 6.

- After the players get a sense of the ball control skills, you quickly want to incorporate these skills into a game. Players should have fun while they're practicing.

- In Superheroes you toss the ball to every player.

- Kickball is another fun game that forces kids to get the ball under control.

Scrimmage

- You should end practice with a regular soccer scrimmage. The game is a great teacher.

- If you want to tie the scrimmage into your practice theme, you can give a team points for every time it does a great job with ball control.

- Make sure you don't stop the game too often to instruct. Occasionally it's appropriate, but for the most part you want to just let the kids play.

MORE FOR YOUNG CHILDREN
A sample practice touches on all the soccer skills by playing games

The practice on page 192 centered on a theme, using different games to work on one specific skill. The practice in this spread touches on a variety of soccer skills. Although it may not produce instant improvement in one aspect of soccer, it will advance the players as a whole.

Many coaches of the youngest children prefer to just play a bunch of silly games and assume that the soccer skills will develop on their own. There is absolutely nothing wrong with this philosophy, and in fact it might in the long run be the better way to go. With this philosophy, you're just building a love of soccer and a familiarity with the ball and how it moves. Although this method doesn't teach any specific skills, it does create more gamelike situations than does just doing a specific skill in isolation.

Because you're not focusing on a specific skill with this type of practice, you'll want to have just a list of games to play.

Warm-up

- If you play Follow the Leader as soon as kids start to arrive, you can get them moving while you're waiting for everyone else to show up.

- You should start out as the leader, but then you can have the last player in line dribble up to the front and become the new leader.

- If you change leaders frequently, you'll have total buy-in because all the kids will want a turn.

- As players trickle in, they join the line. Keep playing until everyone has arrived.

Games and Drills

- Move on to Driving School. This game is silly and fun and gets players in a great mood.

- Now you can sneak in a teaching moment. You might want to teach kids how to do throw-ins or show them a game scenario like goal kicks, for instance.

- Now switch back to a silly game such as Bulldogs. Make sure you bark and growl.

Make sure this is a long list. Most of the games are fun only for a short period of time. Also, many of the games involve the coach and can be exhausting. You'll want to switch things up a lot.

Don't worry about using up all your games in one practice. Kids this age love repetition, so you can do the same games in the same order at the next practice, and they'll think that's great. It also saves on teaching time. And just because you're bored with a game doesn't mean the kids are.

A variation on Ouch! is Animal Ball. When a player hits the coach, instead of the coach yelling, "Ouch," the player gets to pick what type of animal the coach has to be. The coach then has to be that animal for about thirty seconds, and then he gets up and runs around again until someone else hits him.

More Games and Drills

- Little kids mean little attention spans, so having a long list of games and drills is important.

- Move on to "Ouch," which usually can last only as long as the coach can keep running. When this drill is over, it's a good time to stop for a water break for all.

- Tag and Relay races can round out the list.

End with a Scrimmage

- No matter which type of practice you're using, you most likely want to end with a scrimmage.

- If you have a lot of players on your team, you can start with two smaller scrimmages. If you have twelve players, then do two scrimmages of three on three.

- Finally, do a full-team scrimmage.

195

7- TO 10-YEAR-OLD PRACTICE

This sample practice is structured around the theme of dribbling

Being prepared for practice can make all the difference. Young kids have a tendency to create their own entertainment if the coach has too much downtime, either trying to figure out what to do next or trying to figure out how to explain a drill. So make a list, make sure that you understand the drills you're going to teach and, make sure that you have a well-thought-out plan for practice.

The practice offered here is focused on dribbling. But don't be afraid to change it. If the players are having fun and are engaged and enthusiastic about a drill, you may want to keep it going longer than you originally planned, especially if the drill is a productive one. If the drill, however, is not especially fruitful—but merely getting an enthusiastic response because it's a fun game—then you might want to move on to the next item in your practice plan.

Don't feel compelled to have a new set of drills for every

Warm-up

- Because you're focusing on dribbling, have the warm-up include dribbling. First have the players dribble around the field.

- After they're warm, they should do some stretching.

- Now have them do dribbling Rat Races, doing drag-backs at each line.

Dribbling Drills

- Initially you want to teach the players some dribbling skills and then gradually increase the intensity. Go from basic dribbling to running while dribbling to game-level dribbling with defensive pressure.

- Now it's time to do something a little silly although still dribbling based. Criss Cross is a great drill to use here. It's not a game, but because players inevitably are going to bump into each other, they'll have some fun.

- You can find all the dribbling drills in Chapter 5.

practice. Repetition is good. Have the players play the same game for a few weeks, especially if it appears that they like it. Not only will they appreciate doing a drill they like, but also as they become more comfortable with the drill or game, they will take more risks. For instance, if they're doing a dribbling drill, the first couple of times their attention will be focused on doing the drill itself properly. After they learn the drill and don't have to think about that, they can focus on adding a fancy piece of footwork to their dribbling.

Dribbling Games

- After you get the basics of whatever particular dribbling skill you are focusing on—executing drag-backs, keeping the ball close, and so forth—then you can move into some fun games.

- Red Rover, Marauder, and Kings/Queens are all per- fect for this age group.

- You can play these games over and over if the kids seem to like them. Don't worry about trying to get a variety of games.

Scrimmage

- As always, end with a scrimmage. Don't stop the game, but you can shout out advice as the kids are playing.

- Because this was a dribbling-focused scrimmage, you may want to point out when the kids should do a drag-back or an "L" turn. You may want to tell them to keep the ball closer when they're dribbling or to try to shield the ball.

- If you want, tell the kids that they can't shoot on goal unless one player has already tried a move.

ANOTHER SAMPLE PRACTICE
This game-centered practice has instruction in corner kicks

Most kids are playing soccer because they love the game, so it's unpleasant for a coach to stop the momentum and enthusiasm that are usually present in a game or a scrimmage. However, that doesn't mean that you should ignore opportunities that are given to you on a silver platter. Parents and teachers often look for "teachable" moments in life. Coaches should look for "coachable" moments in practice.

In this sample practice, the focus will be on executing cor-

ner kicks in addition to just generally playing the game of soccer. Because the players are young, they're not going to have a consistent kicker lofting the ball to the far post, so each time they practice, something different is going to happen. This might be a coachable moment. It's okay to stop the drill and ask them for feedback. What could they have done with this short kick? What could they do differently so the other team doesn't score? Not every moment of prac-

Warm-up

- Because players tend to trickle in, start the kids who arrive early on a warm-up drill while they're waiting for everyone else to arrive.

- Have them throw the ball up into the air and control it with different parts of their bodies.

- After everyone is there, make the drill tougher by having them start on the ground, throw the ball up, and stand up and control it.

- Juggling is another good filler at the beginning of practice.

Games

- Now play a few games to have fun. You can start by doing some circle dribbling, for instance. Anyone who goes off the circle is out and has to juggle.

- Pick out one of the other fun games, such as Red Rover or Spud.

- End with dribbling races to exhaust the kids before instruction.

tice needs to involve ball movement. Sometimes getting the players to think about the game can be just as valuable.

You don't have to limit this opportunity to scrimmages; you may want to create more opportunities for a corner kick to happen.

Corner Kicks

- Divide the group in half. One half is defense, and the other is offense.

- Let every player on the offense team try at least one corner kick.

- Switch offense and defense and do the same for the other group.

- It's good for all of the kids to know where to stand and how to react both offensively and defensively.

Scrimmage

- Because you're working on corner kicks, you can alter the rules a bit to suit your needs.

- For instance, every time the ball goes over the end line during scrimmage, it's brought in with a corner kick rather than a goal kick.

- Or, if you were working on direct kicks and a wall, you can randomly blow your whistle for a direct kick, whether there's been a foul or not.

PRACTICE FOR 11- TO 14-YEAR-OLDS

This practice is designed to improve transition strategy

By the time the players are eleven to fourteen, most know how to do each of the individual skills. Some may perform better than others, but they're at least familiar with the idea of passing, ball control, dribbling, shooting, and so forth. Nonetheless, ball work and skill sessions are still a vital part of practice. Even professional soccer players still work on the basics to ensure perfect execution time and again, so you can be confident that eleven-year-olds still need that work, too.

On the flip side, however, these players are now ready to move on to the more complex side of soccer and the big-picture aspects of the game. You're probably eager to move on as well if you've been coaching the players for a number of years. They need to work on transitioning, switching fields, and moving and passing to open spaces. These skills aren't going to be learned in little skill sessions and fun games. They involve a different type of practice.

Warm-up

- In this practice, you're trying to teach your players about transition. This practice involves both tackling on defense and outlet passing, so choose drills that focus on these skills for warm-up.

- Divide players into partners. Have them do one-on-one dribbling and defense across the field.

- Now that their muscles are warm, they should stretch.

- Next, you can run a quick passing drill before teaching transition.

Transition Instruction

- Now it's time to teach transition. Give the players a general overview of the concept of transition and what you expect of them.

- Now use one of the drills on page 166.

- Don't try to introduce a bunch of drills at the same time that you're introducing a new concept.

When you have a practice that involves teaching one of these big-picture concepts, you should make sure that the drills and games surrounding the instruction are fun. Start with something fun and physical. If you exhaust the kids, then they'll be more likely to stand still and listen to instruction. Talk about what you're trying to teach and play a half-field scrimmage to illustrate it. Feel free to stop the scrimmage frequently to reinforce the idea.

Then you want to end on a high note. If you know the kids love a certain game, then make it the last thing they do at every practice. They won't want practice to stop, and they'll climb into the car at the end telling their parents how much fun practice was—even if a good chunk of it was deadly dull.

Scrimmage Time

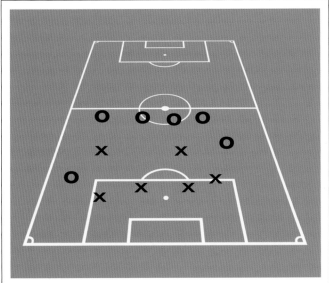

- Begin with a half-field scrimmage, so you can create the situation you're trying to teach.

- In this case, every time the players do a transition successfully, applaud them but let the play continue.

- Stop the play when they do it erroneously.

- Move on to a full-field scrimmage. Let this one play out unless there's a truly egregious error.

Power and Finesse

- Power and Finesse is usually a sure winner with the players, so it's a great one to end with.

- The game is described on page 95.

- There's a lot of competition and not much running,

and most players feel that they have a chance to win despite not being the strongest on the team.

- If the game ends quickly, the players can play it twice.

ANOTHER SAMPLE PRACTICE

This practice is designed to hone mechanical skills

There's something called a "cone of learning" that educators find helpful in imparting a skill to their students. Students remember a small portion of what they hear, a slightly larger portion of what they see, and a considerably larger portion of what they actually do. And apparently they remember virtually all of what they teach.

Coaches can use this learning theory to help them teach soccer skills. You can talk about a specific skill, such as a drag-back, for example, but that's the least effective way to get the information across. Demonstrating isn't enough either. The best way is to first have the kids practice it on their own and walk them individually through each step.

When they've mastered it, then have them teach it to another player who might not have completely mastered it. The "teachers" will have that particular skill cemented into their brain by the end of practice.

Warm-up

- Some coaches like to pick a warm-up drill and stick with it for every practice, regardless of what they're working on that day.

- The kids are old enough to be able to initiate the warm-up as soon as they arrive, without waiting for the coach to lead them.

- The kids will get their muscles warm quickly because they know the drill without thinking, and you won't waste valuable time explaining something that's mere warm-up.

Focusing on a Skill

- Tell the players that you're focusing on a specific skill or two this practice. If they know your focus, it will help them with their own focus.

- You usually can create a relay race that works the skill you're trying to focus on.

- Pick out a few other games in this book that support whatever skill you've chosen.

If you find that someone is having trouble executing a concept—such as the give and go or a through ball—see if she can explain it to the group. After she has to really give it some thought, it may become clearer to her on the field.

If that seems overwhelming, then dial it back a little. Walk through the process with her. Talk about why you're doing each step. A little investment in time during practice will really pay off in the game.

Moving off the Ball

- Now you can work on a more abstract skill, such as moving to the open space.

- Use the four-cones drill on page 162.

- Make sure the defender is really trying to get the ball because that's what creates the intensity in the drill.

Game Time

- As always, you want to end with something fun.

- Because this practice has been so skill heavy, you should end with a scrimmage rather than a game.

- Sometimes it can be fun to have the coaches play in the scrimmage, too.

LOOKING FOR THE BEST
Figure out the assessment style that plays to your strengths

There are two tryout methods: group and individual. For the individual method, you want to figure out which skills you're going to evaluate, and then you evaluate every player based on each of these skills. There may be twenty you identify, or perhaps you care about only ten. But each player gets assessed in a very specific way. Here's a suggested list of skill sets:

Speed, agility, endurance, effort, likeability, coachability, dribbling, faking, passing, moving without the ball, receiving balls on the ground, taking balls out of the air, lofted balls, hooting, heading, throw-ins, individual defense, containment, clearing the ball, team defense.

The difficulty with this method is that oftentimes it highlights players who are quick and have good foot skills, but they might not have good field sense. It's hard to find your top defenders during tryouts. These players frequently don't end up with a high score.

Aggressiveness

- Look for fighters. You want players who use their body as a tool to muscle their way into a possession.

- Don't overvalue foot skills if players are not aggres-sive. They'll have the ball so rarely that their skills become a nonissue.

- Look for players who are frequently on the ground.

Speed

- You can't underestimate speed. You need to have fast attackers who can outsprint the opponent's defenders, and you need to have fast defenders who can stay with the other team's fast attackers.

- Do several types of speed drills. Do short burst runs and longer sprints.

- Also look for bursts of speed during the scrim-mage portion.

For the group method, you divide the players into high, medium, and low groups for every assessment drill or scrimmage that you do. Although this method is not as specific an assessment, you are likely to get a more accurate, although broader, picture of the players.

At the end of each drill, you mark down whether the player was in the high, medium, or low group for that drill. You should also have the players scrimmage and shift them into those three groups as well. At the end of tryouts, you'll hope to find a group whose members are consistently in the high group.

·········· GREEN ● LIGHT ··········

When you're looking for speed, you want to see the players run when they're fresh and when they're tired. Do two speed assessments—one at the beginning and one at the end—because what you really want is the kid who is still fast at the end of the game.

Drive

- Some players instinctively know how to win. That knowledge is rarely something you can teach, but it's invaluable to have on a team.

- Choose this type of player over a more highly skilled

one because skills can be taught but drive can't.

- Look for players who follow their shot into the goal.

- Look for players who are leaders and who boost their teammates' confidence.

Big Picture

- Some children just have an intuitive sense of the game, and this sense shouldn't be undervalued.

- Look for the players who are leading other players with their passes.

- Look for players who are moving to the open spaces.

- Players who don't have the big picture in mind may not get the ball, no matter what their skills might be in a drill.

11- TO 14-YEAR-OLD TRYOUTS
Assess both individual skills and team strengths

Eleven is usually the age when leagues move from small-sided fields to large-sided fields and from eight players on a side to eleven. Because of this fact, even if you're keeping teams together, you're really going to need tryouts to determine who moves on to the expanded team.

For the older players, you don't have to be sneaky about your assessments. They know the score now, and presumably they've been through tryouts. Run drills that show you exactly what you need to know and spend lots of time on scrimmaging.

At this age, too, the kids' personalities and social scenes are going through transformations. These are factors that you also need to consider. Generally, the team with the best athletes is often the team with the most wins, so that's certainly important, but there are other intangible factors to keep in mind that can affect how your team performs.

Rat Race

- This is the drill in which players sprint to one line, touch it, sprint back to the end line, touch it, sprint to the next-farther line, and so forth.

- This sprinting exercise exposes not only your speedy players but also those who combine speed and agility.

- Have the players run short and long races. Full-field races will also give you a sense of who can be speedy only in short bursts and who can maintain speed over distance.

Keep Away

- Put five players on the outside and two in the middle. The five players on the outside pass the ball around the perimeter and through the circle, keeping it away from the two in the middle.

- You'll get a sense of how your players work defen-sively by watching the anticipation and confrontation skills of the two in the middle.

- You'll get a sense of your passers by seeing who takes advantage of a through pass when it's given to them.

As a coach, you'll have to like your players as individuals and your team as a whole. Look for players who get along with other players and recognize the value of playing as a team.

Look for players who are positive and supportive and who are willing to work hard to improve. Kids who don't take responsibility for their own failures but instead focus on the mistakes and failures of others can poison an entire team.

Players who are coachable but unskilled may be at a disadvantage early on but will quickly surpass those who never listen and therefore never improve.

••••••••••••••••• RED ● LIGHT •••••••••••••••

When going from a small-sided team to a large-sided team, you have to be really careful before you move a player down. You're taking so many new kids onto the team that you can probably find room for that one player.

Perimeter Passing

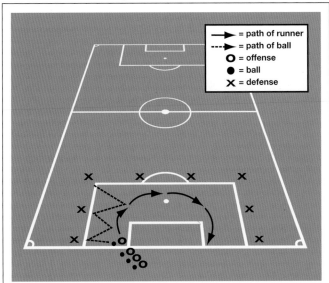

= path of runner
= path of ball
O = offense
● = ball
X = defense

- Divide the players in half. One group lines up around the perimeter of the penalty box. The other group has the balls.

- Have the members of the group with the balls pass to the first player. They receive

the ball back and pass to the next player on the perimeter, moving around the whole box.

- After the first player has moved on to the second perimeter passer, the next player in line can go.

Game Time

- Nothing will tell you more than a scrimmage.

- Have the kids play a few small-sided games with different teammates.

- Now have a big scrimmage. Shift player positions around.

- If you are looking at a couple of players in particular, try them with different players as well.

TRYOUTS

211

GOALKEEPER TRYOUTS

Not every league bothers with goalkeeper tryouts, but here are some tips if you want to do this

Holding tryouts specifically for the goalkeeper position is a little tricky. At the youngest levels, everyone wants to be the goalkeeper. It sounds glamorous to be the only player allowed to use hands. But then after they actually get into the goal, kids find it either boring or discouraging. And that's the end of your large stable of goalkeepers.

There are, however, a few diehards. Oddly enough, they almost always come in one of two categories: (1) the ones who are very good and aggressive and choose to be keepers because they were meant to be goalkeepers and (2) the ones who find refuge in the goal because they are either uncoordinated or lazy and find the field play unsatisfying.

Preparation

- It's a little unfair to judge a player by his equipment, but if a player shows up with goalie gloves and goalie pants or shorts, then you can be sure that this is someone with experience. This factor could be a plus.

- On the flip side, just because a player looks like a keeper doesn't mean that he's any good.

- As long as a good athlete shows interest, you could probably train him to be a good keeper.

Situations

- Do several one-on-one breakaways to see how well players grasp the timing of it all.

- Put them into corner kick situations to see how they take charge of the team.

- Have them dive for balls.

- Test their tipping, punching, punting, and throwing skills.

Even if you find a player who falls into the first category, you absolutely need to play him on the field as well. This is true of both tryouts and the season. Goalkeepers need to understand the play in the field in order to know how to direct their players from the goal mouth. The more experience the keeper can have on the field, the more he'll be able to recognize the field players' limitations and abilities.

When you test your keepers in tryouts, focus on game situations. Feed them high balls, balls in the corner, direct kicks, breakaways, and corner kicks. Don't worry about testing the keepers on penalty kicks. They come up so rarely, and they are such an impossible situation for a goalkeeper that you can save your time and energy in tryouts by avoiding that whole area.

Working the Crowd

- Look for a keeper who takes charge. When there's a crowd in front of the goal, you need to have someone directing the show.

- He should yell, "Keeper" if he's going to get the ball or "Away" if he's not able to.

- You can't use someone who is embarrassed to yell.

Game Situation

- Ultimately, you're going to have to see the keepers in action. Put them into a game and watch what they do. Are they aggressive? Do they hold back? Do they communicate?

- Mix them up with different teams. A good team may mask a weak keeper.

- Look for keepers who will still dive for a ball even if they're unlikely to save it.

213

PLAYER EVALUATION

A number of pieces need to fall into place when you put a team together

After tryouts take place, the age groups will meet to form the teams. This meeting should include all the coaches from the specific age group plus a facilitator who typically is either a board member of the club or someone from the tryout committee. It is important that the facilitator is sensitive to player movement but also stays focused on the ultimate goal of creat-

ing teams tiered by ability. You shouldn't move players if you don't have to, but sometimes you have a new player who really needs to find a spot on the top team, and you're going to have to address the issue. Be careful when you move someone. You don't want to move him back up (or down) the very next year. For the child's sake, try not to let him be a Ping-Pong ball, mov-

Team Needs

- Goalkeepers
- Speedy players for wings and defense
- Passers for midfield
- Aggressive players for defense and strikers

List of Names

- ❑ AnnaMaria
- ❑ Vanessa
- ❑ Alyssa
- ❑ Taylor
- ❑ Bryce
- ❑ Samantha
- ❑ Caity
- ❑ Nina P.
- ❑ Dara
- ❑ Nina K.
- ❑ Eva
- ❑ Minki
- ❑ Jade
- ❑ Lauren
- ❑ Karen
- ❑ Kayla

- If you're evaluating players for their individual skills, then you should make a spreadsheet, with the names down one side and the skills down the other.

- Come up with a simple rating system—perhaps 1 through 5—and rate each player on those skills as he comes up.

- Later you can use all this information to put together a well-rounded team.

- The downside to this method is that it's more complicated, and you may overvalue or undervalue a player in an area.

ing back and forth between two teams. At the older ages, try-outs tend to be used only for players who are new to town or to the program. Coaches will have a better sense of which players aren't cutting it on the top team or which players are excelling on the B team, and are a better resource than an evaluation from a short tryout period. In addition, a coach on a top team in the league may not be looking for merely another top player. The next-best player might be a forward, but this coach has plenty of forwards and really needs to beef up the defense. At this age, it's okay to choose a player based on position.

Group Method

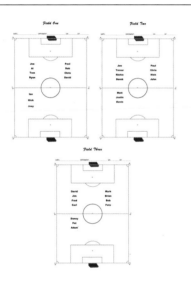

- Set up three fields and divide the players equally but randomly.

- At the end of a drill or a set amount of time, move the best three or four players "up" a field. Move the weakest "down" a field.

- Do this a few times, and eventually you'll have the three fields divided into three levels of play.

- You can do this for both drills and scrimmages.

Communication

- When you talk to the parents and kids, both at the beginning and end of tryouts, you should be as up front as possible.

- Tell them how many players you'll be looking for and explain to them that what they value may not jibe with what you value.

- Do your homework so you can be very specific as to how and when you'll notify them about who is on the team.

TRYOUTS

215

RULES

Soccer is the same around the world except when it comes to indoor play

When you coach indoor soccer, you may encounter some rule changes that you weren't expecting. Essentially the game is the same, but each league and each facility has its own rules, and if you don't know them you could find yourself at a disadvantage. Something as simple as wearing improper footgear could eliminate your entire team if you don't warn your players ahead of time. After you decide to play indoors, the first thing you should do is to educate yourself on the specific rules as they pertain to your league.

For instance, what are the rules for your goalkeepers? Some leagues insist on throws only. Some allow kicks and throws but limit the distance that they can go—with midfield usu-

Clock

- The timing of everything is much faster indoors.

- The games unquestionably are much shorter, and there's usually only about three minutes between the games.

- The time is running time, frequently with no halftime break, although the games may switch sides halfway through.

- The restarts are faster for many reasons: free sub rules, no chasing of balls, and so forth.

Keeper Variations

- Before you sign your keeper up for indoor play, make sure there's a spot for him. Some leagues have much smaller, open goals.

- If your indoor league does use keepers, however, this practice can be tremendous. The keeper will have a lot more opportunities for saves, and because the field is small, situations in front of the goal will come up more often.

- Keepers also may have restrictions on how to release the ball.

ally being the limit. Not only do you need to know this, but you might need to work with your keeper either on developing throwing skills or limiting the kicks. A high punter could have a serious disadvantage with a low ceiling.

Many indoor leagues allow for free substitution. If you're playing in a league with this option, there might be strategies or advantages to subbing more often.

Some indoor leagues don't have offsides. This fact is something else to consider. Is it worth playing short on the defensive end to have one "cherry picker" hanging down by the goal? If the other team comes to this conclusion, how does that change your defensive strategy?

In other words, a little research combined with a lot of thought and analysis beforehand can go a long way. You don't want to arrive at your first game and be surprised. Not only will you be penalized for illegal actions, but also you'll be burned when your defense tries to do an offsides trap and instead gives the other team a breakaway.

Inbounding

- Some indoor leagues keep the inbounding the same—throw-ins, goal kicks, corner kicks, and so forth.

- Others have different rules because the size is so dramatically reduced. For instance, they might require that a player pass the ball on the ground to get it in rather than execute a throw or a lofted kick.

- Others have no inbounding rules because there are no sidelines. Balls are played off the wall.

Subbing

- Just as outdoor leagues have different rules for subbing, so do indoor leagues. They'll all be different, so make sure you understand the subbing rules for the league you're playing in.

- Some leagues have the same subbing rules as outdoor soccer, in which you have to notify the referee.

- Other indoor leagues allow you to sub more like in hockey, just sending players in and out whenever you want.

WHY CHOOSE INDOOR?

The pros and cons of extending the season into the winter

There's a trend in the United States—one that's been entrenched for some time—of having athletes play a single sport year around, and youth soccer is leading the charge in this trend. And if a team is in a state where the winters get cold, snowy, rainy, and muddy, then the team can't plan on much of an outdoor off-season. Enter indoor soccer to fill the gap.

There are differing opinions on whether indoor soccer is a positive for the sport. Most everyone can agree that forcing a child to commit to a single sport at a young age is a mistake for all but a few exceptional players, so it's important for a coach to realize that off-season will be much more low key than the regular season. Not only do you want to prevent burnout, but also many of your players will play several sports at once and will have scheduling conflicts, so you should plan on less of a commitment from your players.

Brain Train

- Because there are fewer players on the indoor team, each player will have more touches on the ball.

- Players also have to think more about the placement and touch of the ball because a big kick will merely send the ball out of bounds.

- At the same time, they're going to have to think quickly because the venue is so much smaller that opponents will be on them faster. It will be hard to find that open run down the wing when they're indoors.

Speed and Agility

- Because of the small size of the facility that you're usually playing in, the transitions happen much more often. Constantly switching back and forth from offense to defense and vice versa is excellent training for outdoor soccer.

- The different surface usually accelerates the game.

- Players will have to react quickly—usually with a one-touch pass—because the game is so much faster.

But don't be discouraged. Winter soccer has its advantages. Even though the season will be less intense, the game itself is faster and smaller, giving your players lots of touches on the ball. And if the players keep touching the ball year around, doing that will at least maintain their skills and hopefully improve them.

On the other hand, playing a sport year round takes some of the glow off. It's hard to get excited about the arrival of soccer season if it's always soccer season. Also, many coaches feel that their players become better athletes by playing a variety of sports rather than playing one exclusively.

Ultimately, you have to figure out what works for you. But if you do decide to provide an indoor option for your team, you should make sure that the off-season play is both voluntary and fun.

Keeper Skills

- In outdoor soccer eleven players are on the field, so frequently coaches are able to overload their defense, which prevents the ball from ever getting to the keeper.

- In indoor soccer there are fewer players, so the keeper sees a lot more action.

- In addition, because the space is smaller, even defensive players are occasionally in position to take shots on goal.

- All this extra experience will really help your keeper's game.

Weather

- Indoor soccer allows players to practice in all weather conditions, which can get you an edge on other local teams that have to bow to the whims of weather.

- Even if you're competitive with local teams, your players may not keep up with players in other parts of the country (or world) where it's warm and sunny all the time.

- Also, if rain keeps your muddy field constantly out of play, you're out of luck. Indoor soccer solves that problem.

FORMATIONS
Choose the right indoor formation for your team

Most indoor games are eight on eight, but some leagues might have different sizes. Before you make any decisions on where to play you need to check with the league to find out what the team size is. After you have that number, you should pick a formation that aligns best with what you play during the regular season. The four mentioned here are the four most common and match up with the most common outdoor formations.

Of course, it's not a requirement that your indoor team match your outdoor team. You may find yourself without a key player in the winter, and you'll have to adapt to that. Frequently indoor teams won't be able to field the full team from outdoors due to other commitments.

If your goalkeeper is the one who is missing, you may want to consider different factors than you'd consider if you were looking to develop an outdoor keeper. If you don't already

2-3-2

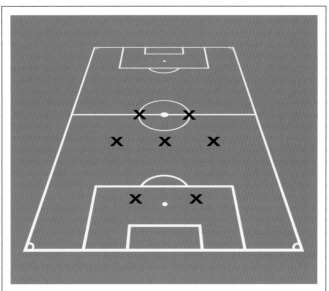

- For this formation, you'll have two defenders, three midfielders, and two attackers.

- This formation matches well with the 4-4-2 because the outside midfielders have to

make long runs and still get back for defense.

- Also, the attackers in this formation will be moving the same way as they would with the 4-4-2.

3-2-2

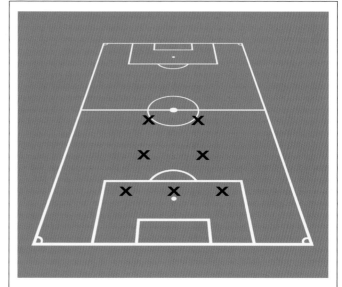

- For this formation, you'll have three defenders, two midfielders, and two forwards.

- This formation works well for a team that needs to focus on the defense playing together.

- Both defensively and offensively it would match up with either a 4-3-3 or a 4-4-2.

have a keeper, then you should look for the players who already have quick hands. This is the key to indoor play. Outdoor keepers need to be strong. Indoor keepers need to be quick.

If, on the other hand, you are lucky enough to have carried your regular goalkeeper into the indoor season, then you can be happy with the training she'll be getting. Even if she doesn't start out with quick hands, indoor practice will really help with her reaction time. Prepare her for the fact that she'll get a whole lot more action and the fact that the games will probably be higher scoring. It might be depressing at first, but she'll have to learn to accept and recognize the short-term pain for long-term gain.

2-2-3

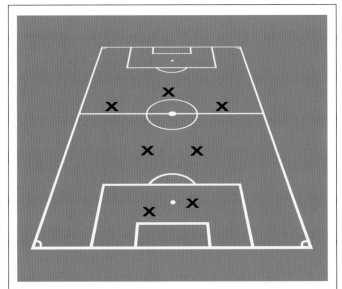

- For this formation, you'll have two defenders, two midfielders, and three forwards.

- This formation works well for a team that wants to focus on a three-forward offensive line.

- This formation aligns best with a 4-3-3 formation.

1-3-3

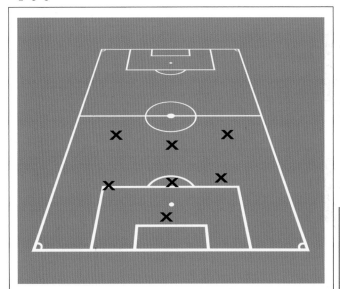

- For this formation, you'll have one defender—who will be a sweeper—three midfielders, and three forwards.

- This formation works well for a team that needs to work on the sweeper controlling the defensive play.

- It also reinforces your wings having to get back on defense.

- It aligns best with any formation that uses a sweeper.

INDOOR DRILLS
Adapt your practices to suit the specific indoor venue

Indoor soccer is a quick game. The space is small, and the ball changes direction constantly. It's a great way to improve the reactions of all your players. Your players will also have a lot more touches on the ball, which should help with their skills.

The downside is that some of the big picture of outdoor soccer can sometimes get lost in indoor soccer. Chipping over the defense or playing the ball to an open space are both almost nonexistent. Strength and power are practically worthless indoors, whereas finesse and individual skills shine.

All of this means that when you practice, you should focus on drills that work on small-space ball movement and individual skills. Not only is this what players will be using when they play indoors, but also it provides an extra challenge that will take their skills to the next level. If a player can control

Using the Wall

- Now that more indoor facilities are being built, there are fewer indoor soccer leagues that play in an environment where a wall is in play.

- However, if you do find yourself in an indoor league that uses a wall, you'll need

- to practice using it to your advantage.

- The wall can be a useful give-and-go tool.

- Stronger players might be able to use the wall to cross the ball into the center of the field.

One-touch Passing

- One-touch passing and scoring are paramount in indoor soccer. Your players need to practice these plays as much as anything else.

- A number of one-touch passing drills are described in this book.

- You can also take any other drill and adapt it to focus on one-touch passing and shooting.

a ball rolling on a hard wooden floor, then he certainly can control one on a field.

The quality and types of indoor spaces will also dictate what you do in practice. If you're in an indoor soccer facility, then you have more options than if you're in a high school gymnasium. The further you get away from the game of outdoor soccer, the more you'll have to focus your practice on individual skills.

Quick Feet

- Have two lines on the ground, about 20 feet apart. The players should pair up.

- One partner in each pair stands on one line with a ball. The other partner stands about 5 feet away with his legs apart.

- The first player passes the ball through the legs of his partner. The partner has to wait until the ball goes through his legs, and then he must turn and race after the ball and catch it before it reaches the other line.

Two-goal Shooting

- If the goals are light, you can bring the two goals close together and have a shooting fest.

- Doing this really helps the players react quickly and take lots of shots.

- It also teaches them that they don't have to wait for the perfect shot or be completely open before they try to score.

RUNNING A PRACTICE

Because you don't have any flexibility with field time, you should come prepared and start on time

Most indoor time is paid for by the team, and it's generally not cheap. The indoor spaces are usually highly scheduled, and you have your hour to move in quickly, get the job done, and move out.

Be sure to make it clear to your players and parents that they should arrive fifteen minutes early to practice. Doing this

gives players time to get all their equipment on, their shoelaces tied, and their heads in the right places. (It also means that the few people who are always late will still be on time for the actual practice.) Depending on what the waiting area is like in your indoor space, you can also have the players do a little warm-up and some stretching while they're waiting so

Warm-up

- Although warm-up is important in an outdoor practice, it's something that can be sacrificed in an indoor practice.

- Think of a drill that works to get your players moving and the blood pumping but

also works on whatever skill you're focusing on.

- After this drill, your players can do some short stretches while you go over the plan for the session or discuss some strategy.

Drill Time

- Indoor soccer training is to hone individual skills more than big team concepts and strategies.

- Choose drills that work on footwork, speed, or agility.

- Turn up the intensity on a drill by requiring one-touch passing.

you don't have to waste valuable time during practice.

Have one or two specific ideas about which skills or strategies you want to work on. Figure out some good drills to highlight those skills or strategies. It's better if your players are already familiar with the drills because again you don't want to take up precious time with a lot of explanation.

After you're done drilling, then move on to scrimmages. Start with small-sided scrimmaging, such as a three-on-three, and then move on to full-sided. Obviously the full-sided will be smaller than a regular outdoor game anyway. Use the first part of the scrimmage to stop and teach, but then just let the kids play at the end.

Let them play right up until your time is up. If you have something to say to your players, wait until the practice is over. You can move them off the field, let the next scheduled group onto the field, and then do your talking and wrap-up in the waiting area.

3 versus 3

- Divide your team into several groups of three.

- Use the whole field for a three-on-three game. The players will be exhausted, so put in new teams after only a few minutes.

- The players get more touches on the ball and find it easy to move to the open spaces.

- They are forced to play both offense and defense and transition constantly.

Game Time

- Make sure you include tons of real scrimmage time in your indoor practices.

- Because your indoor time is presumably supplemental to your regular season, you should be sure to keep it fun and low key.

- Letting players scrimmage for thirty minutes of your sixty-minute time is fine. This is what they enjoy most, and the game itself is a wonderful teacher.

SOCCER CAMPS & CLINICS

The number of soccer camps and clinics in the United States—and all over the world, for that matter—is enormous, but most of them can be grouped into four categories:

1. Local camps and clinics

Many towns across the United States offer local camps and clinics for youth. These are almost always day camps offered by local coaches. They tend be a better bargain for parents, located nearby, and are easily found through local recreation programs or word of mouth. Assistant coaches are frequently high school players, so these are best for the younger set.

2. National and international for-profit camps

These can be day camps or sleepaway camps. In the United States, the camps frequently hire soccer players from other countries to serve as coaches and trainers.

3. College camps

These are camps that are usually run by a college soccer coach, frequently employing the team's players as assistant coaches. Coaches earn off-season money and give their programs greater exposure. They are generally, however, not looking at these camps as recruiting programs.

4. Competitive camps that require previous qualification or invitation

These camps are for the top players. These are frequently used by colleges, Major League Soccer (MLS), and the U.S. National team and Olympic development teams for recruiting and for developing top players.

MAJOR LEAGUE SOCCER (MLS)

Major League Soccer is the men's professional soccer organization in the United States. It began in 1996. The season is March to October, and the teams play approximately thirty games in the regular season, more if they make it to the playoffs. For more information on the individual teams, visit the MLS Web site: www.mlsnet.com

Teams:

Eastern Conference:

Eastern Conference:

Chicago Fire

Columbus Crew

D.C. United

Kansas City Wizards

New England Revolution

New York Red Bulls

Toronto FC

Western Conference:

Chivas USA

Colorado Rapids

FC Dallas

Houston Dynamo

Los Angeles Galaxy

Real Salt Lake

San Jose Earthquakes

Seattle begins play in 2009, Philadelphia in 2010; their conference affiliations will be announced later.
To order MLS clothing and equipment, go to www.MLSgear.com.

RESOURCES

OTHER SOCCER ORGANIZATIONS

Aside from Major League Soccer, there are a number of different organizations that might be of interest to both coaches and players. Here are a few of the most popular:

AYSO (American Youth Soccer Organization)

National organization of youth soccer. Established in 1964, it currently has over fifty thousand teams registered. The philosophy emphasizes balanced teams and the "everyone plays" attitude.
www.soccer.org

CONCACAF (Confederation of North, Central America and Caribbean Association Football)

The continental organization that the United States national team play in. FIFA has organized six continental groups to govern World Cup qualifying play.
www.concacaf.com

FIFA (Fédération Internationale de Football Association)

Governing body responsible for establishing and enforcing the rules of soccer. It also runs the World Cup and the European Cup.
www.fifa.com

NISL (National Indoor Soccer League)

The NISL provides professional indoor soccer league play. There are five teams in this league: Philadelphia Kixx, Baltimore Blast, Monterrey LaRaZa, Rockford Rampage, and Massachusetts Twisters.
www.NISLnet.com

USSF (United States Soccer Federation)

The official organization for United States soccer, including the men's and women's national teams.
www.ussoccer.com

USYSA (United States Youth Soccer Association)

National organization of youth soccer. Established in 1974, it currently has over 3.2 million registered players. The teams range from highly competitive Olympic and National Team development programs to less competitive community teams.
www.usyouthsoccer.org

WPS (Women's Professional Soccer)

A new organization that will begin play in 2009 to provide opportunities to play and watch women's soccer in the United States. The league will be made up of seven teams: Bay Area, Boston, Chicago, Los Angeles, New Jersey/New York, St. Louis, and Washington, D.C., with expansion expectations for Philadelphia and Atlanta in 2010.
www.womensprosoccer.com

CHECKLISTS

Even though all of this information is in the book, sometimes it's handy to have a checklist in front of you before you head to practice or a game. Here are a few checklists that you might find useful.

Player Gear

- ❏ ball
- ❏ cleats
- ❏ socks
- ❏ shinguards
- ❏ shorts
- ❏ shirt
- ❏ uniform
- ❏ headgear
- ❏ goalkeeper shirt
- ❏ goalkeeper gloves
- ❏ goalkeeper pants or shorts

Practice Checklist

- ❏ ball bag: an easy way to carry both the balls and the extra equipment
- ❏ cell phone: handy in an emergency
- ❏ cones: can be used for many drills for goals, boundary lines, etc.
- ❏ disks: similar to cones
- ❏ dry erase board: allows the coach to demonstrate strategy
- ❏ dry erase marker: use to write on the dry erase board
- ❏ emergency forms: these usually have contact information and medical information for each player
- ❏ first aid kit: should include bandages and ice packs, among other items
- ❏ pinnies: two colors are helpful in case you want to make more than one team. Reversible ones are great for the same reason.
- ❏ small goals: can be more useful than cones or disks for some drills
- ❏ whistle: allows the coach to get the players' attention

Game Checklist

- ❏ game ball: should be clean and well-inflated
- ❏ ball bag: extra balls are good for warm-up before game.
- ❏ cell phone: handy in an emergency
- ❏ clipboard: keeps papers—rosters, emergency forms, player cards, etc.—all in one place
- ❏ dry erase board: you may need to demonstrate strategy at halftime
- ❏ dry erase marker: use to write on the dry erase board
- ❏ emergency forms: these usually have contact information and medical information for each player
- ❏ first aid kit: should include bandages and ice packs, among other items
- ❏ goalkeeper gloves: good to have a spare, even if your goalkeeper has some
- ❏ goalkeeper shirt: good to have a spare, even if your goalkeeper has one
- ❏ pen or pencil: to make changes in rosters or lineups or make notations
- ❏ pinnies: you may need them if the other team has similar uniforms
- ❏ player cards: required for play in many leagues

Tryouts Checklist

- ❏ ball bag full of balls
- ❏ cell phone: handy in an emergency
- ❏ list of players trying out
- ❏ pen or pencil for notes
- ❏ clipboard: a hard surface to write notes on
- ❏ cones and disks
- ❏ emergency forms: these usually have contact information and medical information for each player
- ❏ first aid kit: should include bandages and ice packs, among other items
- ❏ pinnies: critical, because teams will be constantly changing
- ❏ small goals: can be more useful than cones or disks for some drills
- ❏ whistle: gets the attention of a large group

GLOSSARY

charge: a foul that occurs when a player runs into another player

chip: a kick lifted into the air to get over an opponent

clear: a kick that sends the ball far away from the goal area

cleats: soccer shoes with hard rubber knobs on the soles to prevent slipping

containment: a defensive move designed to slow a dribbler

corner arc: the marked area on all four corners of the field

corner flag: a visual aid placed in the corner to help the referee determine where the ball left the field

corner kick: a restart taken from the corner arc after the defense has kicked the ball over their own end line

dangerous play: when a player plays in a manner that may be dangerous to himself or others

direct kick: a free kick awarded after a foul

dribbling: moving the ball with the feet

double team: when two players defend one attacker

drop ball: a restart in which neither team has the advantage and the referee drops the ball between two opposing players

end line: the line at the end of the field, also called the "goal line"

far post: the post farthest from the ball

give and go: a play in which the ball goes from one player to a teammate, and then the teammate returns the ball to the original player

goalkeeper: the designated player who is allowed to touch the ball with his hands as long as he remains within the designated area

goal kick: a restart taken by a defender after the attackers have kicked the ball over the end line. The ball is placed anywhere within the six yard line.

goal line: see *end line*

half volley: a shot in which the ball is kicked just after it bounces up off the ground

handball: when a player other than the goalkeeper touches the ball with her hands

indirect kick: a free kick awarded after a foul with the restriction that the ball must touch two players before it may enter the goal

instep: the hard, bony area on the top of the foot

juggling: keeping the ball in the air

kickoff: the method of putting the ball into play at the start of each half and after a goal has been scored

marking up: when defender stick with a single player

midfielders: the players who provide a link between offense and defense

obstruction: when a defensive player, instead of going for the ball, uses his body to prevent an opposing player from reaching it

offsides: when a player does not have either the ball or two defenders between herself and the goal

overlap: when a player moves forward from his own positional line in front of someone in the line in front of him

penalty area: the box outlined on the field that is 18 yards out from the goal

penalty kick: a free kick awarded when the defensive team commits a foul within the penalty area

pinnies: loose vests worn over shirts usually in practices to distinguish one team from the other

planting foot: the nonkicking foot

red card: a plastic card displayed by the referee to indicate that a player has been ejected from the game

restart: the act of putting the ball back into play

set play: a restart with a planned strategy

shielding: keeping the body between the defender and the ball

shinguards: required protective gear worn on the lower part of the leg

sideline: the line marking the out-of-bounds along the length of the field

slide tackle: a method of stealing the ball by sliding along the ground

small-sided game: any game that has fewer than eleven players

stopper: the player at the front of the defense

striker: the frontmost attacking player

sweeper: the player who is the last line of defense

through pass: a kick that splits the defenders

throw-in: a restart in which the ball goes over the sideline

touchline: see *sideline*

trap: when a player gets control of a moving ball

volley: a shot in which the ball is kicked while in the air

wall: a defensive tactic in which one to four players line up in front of a direct kick

wall pass: see *give and go*

wing: a player who is positioned out by the sidelines

yellow card: a card shown by the referee to issue a warning to a player who has demonstrated rough or unsportsmanlike behavior

INDEX

INDEX